Blessings!

Bro. Mike

FORGIVE

The Journey Toward Peace

REV. MIKE MARECLE,
Doctor of Ministry in Pastoral Counseling

Introduction

The act of forgiveness has been called a small taste of death.

I can remember feeling that way, that if I were to forgive a certain person, it would be another wound. What would I do with all the hurt he had caused me? Where was the justice in it, my choice to forgive? Where was the fairness? It wasn't my fault, and yet I was expected to forgive.

On the other hand, I had no peace in my life. The emotions of anger and resentment were eating me alive. What was I to do? How could I do what seemed an impossible task—forgive this person?

I never would have believed that God would take me on this journey of forgiveness. But He has. And He continues to do so.

He can do the same for you. I wrote this book to share with you how the Lord gave me peace and purpose in my life through the practice of forgiveness.

Having counseled with thousands of people in tens of thousands of hours at Hope Family Ministries, I've seen a recurring problem: a lack of peace caused by the inability, and refusal, to forgive. I've been blessed to witness radical improvement in the lives of those who were willing to learn and apply these principles and skills.

You are invited to go on a journey with me. If you accept the invitation, you will learn and be challenged to apply what you learn. You won't see mile markers, but you will experience milestones. On the journey there will be things to leave behind and things to pick up along the way. You will also find hope, healing and peace. Peace with God, peace within yourself and peace with other people. Peace with your past, present and future.

If you trust God by applying what you learn, then along the journey God will begin to put new love, joy, peace, patience, kindness, goodness, gentleness, faithfulness and self-control into your life. The pure Fruit of the Spirit comes from the Spirit of God when you are in a proper relationship with Him, a relationship of learning from Him and trusting and obeying Him. Through this He heals you, directs your paths, and blesses you with a clear conscience.

I do hope you will accept the invitation.

If you have unfinished business with God, within yourself or with others, you don't have to remain stuck and forfeit the fullness of God's blessing. And, unfortunately, you can also expect the destruction to continue. You will be fearful without the love you want and need. You will look for happiness externally in people and circumstances. You may be troubled, impatient, mean spirited, vengeful, unkind, ungrateful, unfaithful, harsh and without self-control.

This book is about forgiveness. From my personal journey and Biblical wisdom, I will share the definition of forgiveness and practical steps in the process of forgiving. Experiencing forgiveness changed my life and restored many of my relationships, first with God and then with others. I hope and pray it will change yours.

Sometimes we travel as fast as we can to reach our destination. I encourage you to take time to read this important information. I also challenge you to allow time to rest, reflect and remember what you have learned. I hope and pray you will be blessed as I share my faith journey and God's Word.

Contents

Section I
My Journey of Forgiveness

I didn't realize how much anger and resentment had built up over time. More important, I had never seen how emotionally destructive it was to me and to others in my life. Finally, I came to understand that the "overflow of my heart" was affecting me negatively – and how I could change it.

Anger isn't always a bad emotion – it's all in how we deal with it. I had not learned how to process my anger. I didn't know how to not be angry! Then I learned 14 practical steps to forgive others and process my anger.

I realized I had all kinds of excuses for not forgiving and that the worry, fear and discord in my life was tied up in those excuses. I counted 14 consequences of not forgiving. And I came to terms with the connection between God's forgiveness of me and my forgiveness of others.

I'd been believing the wrong definitions of forgiveness by trusting the thoughts of others and myself. Of course, Satan encouraged my wrong thinking and used it against me. I identified 11 things that were not forgiveness, a process that helped point to God's correct definition, through His Word.

I had not accepted how much destruction I'd brought into my life by being unforgiving. My bitterness ate me up emotionally and my anger alienated those around me. When I began to understand God's view of forgiveness, my life became less disruptive and more helpful to everyone around me.

Section II

Getting Practical with Forgiveness

I desperately needed peace and found it, first, through God's forgiveness through Christ. I gained a new family in the church and I became a new person. I discovered the importance of God's Word to give me rest, show me what God was really like, and who I am, through Him.

Total peace didn't come all at once; it is a journey, after all. I learned how to forgive myself by believing God, through His Word, instead of believing my own mistaken way of thinking.

I still needed to learn how to forgive others in order to claim the peace that surpasses all understanding. I learned it was an act of faith, and that God wanted to give me the very faith I needed for Him to keep working in me as I forgave others. This journey continues.

Section I

My Journey of Forgiveness

Sometimes we get ahead of ourselves.
Sometimes we miss the journey trying to get to the destination.
We somehow conclude that as soon as we discover an expectation,
that expectation should be achieved.
We somehow conclude that as soon as we learn of a destination,
we have to get there as soon as possible.

Immediately.

But that's not the case in our pursuit of peace.
It is a journey, and one which
we will likely travel more than once
in our lives here on planet earth.
This section not only shows my journey
toward forgiveness but, in so doing,
offers you my broken example of healing and restoration.
Apply it as you will.

Let's take the first step on our journey.

Chapter 1

How was unresolved resentment killing me and my relationships?

I used to blow up over little things. I had a short fuse and was known to overreact. Back then, you might think I was a kind, funny and considerate person, especially if we had just met. But people who knew me well painted a very different picture of me. Oh, I didn't explode over just anything in any setting. But certain people could set me off. Unexpected interruptions could set me off. I had a chip on my shoulder, and I didn't even fully know it.

I didn't realize how much resentment had built up, over time.

Why were there such different "sides" of me? In the New Testament of the Bible, James, Chapter 1, talks about a double-minded man. To be double-minded is to attempt to live two lives at one time. James also says the double-minded person is unstable in all he does. One side of me wanted to be relationally healthy and try to do better, while the other side of me was mad as hell and had given up on having healthy relationships. Like most people, I didn't realize how much resentment had built, over time.

At the time, I didn't fully understand that the root of my anger was in unforgiveness. I first needed to see and feel the depth of my unhappiness with myself and my life. As challenging as it was to accept, it was necessary for me to be honest about my anger. I had to "own" my anger and stop blaming others for the devastation I caused in my anger. Secondly, I had to understand exactly how my definition of "normal" compared to what others might perceive as normal.

Often, when counseling with people, I will attempt to convert their answer to a numerical scale. This is to avoid misunderstanding and miscommunication. For example, when I ask how things have been going, "fine" is a common answer. If I ask them to put "fine" on a scale of 1 to 10, with 1 being less fine and 10 being more fine, the word "fine" becomes a 2 for one person and an 8 for another.

In the same way, the meaning of words to describe anger or resentment can vary. In trying to move from subjective (each person's definition) to objective (a commonly agreed upon definition), I often use the following illustration.

Let's say, related to resentment or anger, each person has a range of response that goes from 0 to 10. Zero doesn't mean there is never anger. It does mean that we are up to date, or current, in processing anger or resentment. Ten on this scale means we hit the point of losing it. For each person the concept of "losing it" is going to be a little different. For one person it could be shutting down or numbing out. For another it could be throwing up their hands, mumbling and walking away. For yet another it could be verbal, emotional or physical abuse. Still others would take another pill or drink or get high.

For the sake of illustration, we are up to date in our processing of resentment or anger if we start at zero and have a normal response to the situation. If, however, our starting point is above zero, our response will be greater – proportionate to our starting point.

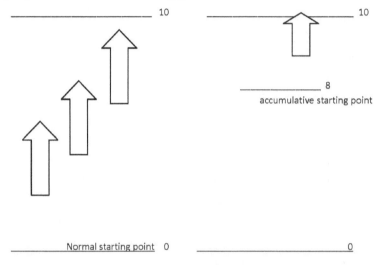

The illustration above shows (left side) someone responding from a healthy starting point.

The illustration above shows (right side) my response starting point by the time I was a teenager. Over time, unresolved resentment and anger accumulated because they don't automatically go away with time. They are residual. The illustration shows that, because forgiveness, anger and resentment were not properly managed, my starting point kept moving up the scale until it reached a level 8. If something happened that should produce a "2-level" response, instead of starting at 0 and going to 2, I started at 8 and went to 10.

While growing up, many times I was asked, "Why do you act like that when you get mad?" People often avoided me because it was "normal" for me to overreact. Do people avoid you because you overreact? Do you shut down or numb out? Do you mumble, throw up your hands and walk away? Do you become abusive? Do you self-medicate?

What is your starting point on the scale?

Long ago, I was diagnosed with high blood pressure. However, with regular checkups and a routine of monitoring myself physically, my condition can be controlled. I can live a fairly normal life.

In the same way, monitoring the condition of my spiritual life is important for spiritual health. We can assess the condition of our spiritual hearts by realizing our choice of words, our attitude and our behavior. It is more important than monitoring the condition of my physical heart for physical health. God's Word guides our assessment. Jesus said *the* condition of our heart is revealed by the overflow of our attitude, words and behavior.

Our level of resentment and anger directly affects our words, attitude and behavior. "For out of the overflow of the heart the mouth speaks. The good man brings out of the good stored up in him, and the evil man brings evil things out of the evil stored up in him." (Matthew 12:34b)

What do your words, attitude and behavior reveal
about the condition of your spiritual heart?

Which of the two lists below best describes your attitude, words and behavior? Would the people who know you best say that you have peace in your life?

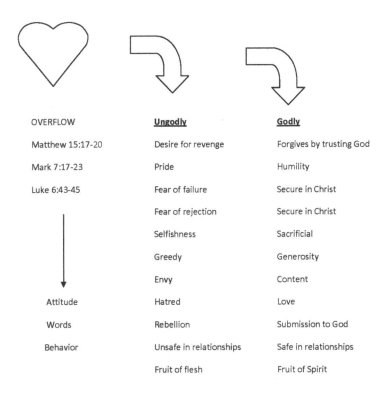

OVERFLOW	**Ungodly**	**Godly**
Matthew 15:17-20	Desire for revenge	Forgives by trusting God
Mark 7:17-23	Pride	Humility
Luke 6:43-45	Fear of failure	Secure in Christ
	Fear of rejection	Secure in Christ
	Selfishness	Sacrificial
	Greedy	Generosity
	Envy	Content
Attitude	Hatred	Love
Words	Rebellion	Submission to God
Behavior	Unsafe in relationships	Safe in relationships
	Fruit of flesh	Fruit of Spirit

As you read the lists above, you might think, "Well, now I feel even worse because I've got a whole lot of ungodly reactions!" Do not despair; we aren't going to leave you at this place of feeling guilty. This book will move through the process of filling our hearts with godly actions and reaction, by faith, through Christ. Remember, this is a process of surrender, not "becoming better" in our own power.

**Ask God to allow you to hear and see the
overflow of your heart!**

A little poetry, if you please:

*Why someone blows up over little things is very confusing;
often they don't realize the need for defusing.
When we explode it seems foolish to say
that when we look back we don't know why we acted that way.
It is possible to appear full of contentment,
when under the surface we are filled with resentment.
Living in resentment is very draining.
To deal with it God's way requires some training.
If I don't yield to Him I'll be back in sin,
be caught in a battle that I cannot win.
God says don't let the sun go down on your wrath,
or you will surely continue down the wrong path.
The devil will use it to set a stronghold of lies;
without my knowledge, he will cover my eyes.
I'll be joining the devil in a life of destruction,
and continue to wonder why I have such eruptions.*

I learned that forgiveness is the foundational component to manage the resentment and anger in my life and relationships. I also learned that I lacked the knowledge and skills to process anger and resentment.

In one of my educational adventures, I had the opportunity to select a research topic. I chose the emotion of anger, not only because of my struggle with anger, but also because I live in a world with many angry people. Let's continue our journey in the next chapter. We'll explore the causes and options for dealing with anger.

Chapter 2

What caused my anger?
How did I become a safe person?

Years ago, I may not have fully understood the importance of forgiveness. But I knew one thing: I was angry. And my anger kept leading to more anger. My emotional life seemed out of control and continually sabotaging my hope for peace and happiness. I hated being angry, but found myself unable to control it.

My problem with anger had three components. First, I did not have the knowledge and skills to process anger properly. Secondly, because I did not know how to process anger properly, my anger wasn't processed to closure; I only attempted containment. Finally, I did not ask God for help.

I didn't know how not to be angry.

We will all be faced with situations, big or small, where we will need to forgive an offender. If we don't, we will be saddled with anger that eats up our peace.

Every day we deal with situations that produce the normal God-given emotion of anger (resentment). Those include:

1. When **our goals are blocked**
2. When **we experience injustice**
3. When **we feel threatened**
4. When **we feel guilty**
5. When **others do not honor our morals and values**

During my youth, I learned from three different men how they processed their anger. My exposure included modeling – what I observed, and verbal instruction – what was said to me. Each man modeled and taught me differently, by example and instruction. And none of them gave me the perfect example of how to process my own anger. Therefore, I was stuck in a pattern of anger without any knowledge for how to get rid of my unhealthy expressions of that emotion.

After I became a Christian I allowed my Heavenly Father to model and teach me how to process anger. As I studied the Bible, I saw how God modeled this process, through the example of Jesus and how He processed His emotions. Now, this wasn't an instantaneous occurrence. It took time. And my journey isn't over.

But I did come to understand that there is no better instruction than God's Word. "All Scripture is God-breathed and is useful for teaching, rebuking, correcting and training in righteousness, so that the man of God may be thoroughly equipped for every good work." (2 Timothy 3:16). "Above all, you must understand that no prophecy of Scripture came about by the prophet's own interpretation. For prophecy never had its origin in the will of man, but men spoke from

God as they were carried along by the Holy Spirit." (2 Peter 1:20-21)

The words and stories recorded in the Bible are by God's design. Some of the stories teach. Some of the stories rebuke. Some of the stories correct. Some of the stories train in righteousness. I looked for "teaching moments" in Scripture that showed how to handle anger correctly and what to avoid when choosing how to handle anger. You will find at least one of those in the following illustrations. My purpose in exploring these stories is to demonstrate how people experience the normal God-given emotion of anger (resentment).

Jesus used anger (resentment) to bring about good change.

"People were bringing little children to Jesus to have him touch them, but the disciples rebuked them. When Jesus saw this He was indignant. He said to them, 'Let the little children come to me, and do not hinder them.'" (Mark 10:13-14a) Synonyms of indignant include angry, resentful, infuriated and mad. Jesus wanted children to freely approach Him. The disciples **blocked a goal.** Because His goal was blocked, Jesus experienced the normal God-given emotion of anger (resentment).

The anger Jesus experienced was used to bring about a good change. Jesus provided an example of using the emotion of anger (resentment) in a way that pleases God. How do you respond when a goal is blocked? Is the anger you experience being used to bring about a good change?

Esau used anger (resentment) to plan for revenge.

Genesis 27 records the story of Isaac's preparing to give his blessing to Esau, his firstborn son. Isaac was old and blind. Isaac's wife, Rebekah, wanted Esau's younger brother, Jacob, to receive the blessing that belonged to Esau. Rebekah and Jacob successfully deceived Isaac and he gave Esau's blessing to Jacob. When Isaac told Esau what happened, "he burst out with a loud and bitter cry" (Gen. 27:34). "Esau held a grudge against Jacob because of the blessing his father had given him. He said to himself, 'The days of mourning for my father are near; then I will kill my brother Jacob.'" (Genesis 27:41)

Esau **experienced injustice**, which caused him to have the normal God-given emotion of anger (resentment).

The anger Esau experienced was used to plan for revenge. Esau provided an example of using the emotion of anger (resentment) in a way that did not please God. How do you respond when you experience injustice? Is the anger you experience processed in a way that pleases God?

Elijah used anger (resentment) to judge others and complain.

"Now Ahab told Jezebel everything Elijah had done and how he had killed all the prophets with the sword. So Jezebel sent a messenger to Elijah to say, 'May the gods deal with me, be it ever so severely, if by this time tomorrow I do not make your life like that of one of them.' Elijah was afraid and ran for his life." (1 Kings 19:1-3a) Elijah felt threatened. Later when God approached him, he condemned the Israelites for breaking the covenant. He also bitterly complained over the fruitlessness of his own work. (1 Kings 19:10, 14) When Elijah felt **threatened**, he experienced the normal God-given emotion of anger (resentment).

The anger Elijah experienced was used to judge others and complain. Elijah provided an example of using the emotion of anger (resentment) in a way that did not please

God. How do you respond when you feel threatened? Is the anger you experience processed in a way that pleases God?

Cain used anger (resentment) to mask guilt and to remove his brother.

"Now Abel kept flocks, and Cain worked the soil. In the course of time Cain brought some of the fruits of the soil as an offering to the Lord. But Abel brought fat portions from the firstborn of his flock. The Lord looked with favor on Abel and his offering, but on Cain and his offering he did not look with favor. So Cain was very angry, and his face was downcast. Then the Lord said to Cain, 'Why are you angry? Why is your face downcast? If you do what is right, will you not be accepted?'" (Genesis 4:2b-7a) Cain **felt guilty**, which caused him to experience the normal God-given emotion of anger (resentment).

The anger Cain experienced was used to mask his guilt and to remove his brother. Cain provided an example of using the emotion of anger (resentment) in a way that did not please God. How do you respond to feeling guilty? Is the anger you experience being processed in a way that pleases God?

Moses used anger (resentment) to destroy something and to hurt others.

"Moses turned and went down the mountain with the two tablets of the Testimony in his hands. They were inscribed on both sides, front and back. The tablets were the work of God; the writing was the writing of God, engraved on the tablets. When Joshua heard the noise of the people shouting, he said to Moses, 'There is the sound of war in the camp.' Moses replied: 'It is not the sound of victory, it is not the sound of defeat; it is the sound of singing that I hear.' When Moses approached the camp and saw the calf and the dancing, his anger burned and he threw the tablets out of his hands, breaking them to pieces at the foot of the mountain. And he took the calf they had made and burned it in the fire; then he ground it to powder, scattered it on the water and made the Israelites drink it." (Exodus 32:18-20) While Moses was with God, on Mount Sinai, the impatient Israelites took matters into their own hands. They made and worshiped a golden calf. When Moses realized the **Israelites were not honoring the morals and values** God had given, he experienced the normal God-given emotion of anger (resentment).

The anger Moses experienced was used to destroy something and to hurt others. Moses provided an example of using anger (resentment) in a way that did not please God. How do you respond when your morals and values are not honored? Is the anger you experience being used in a way that pleases God?

One summer I was putting some money back for a special reason. While mowing the lawn I heard a strange, loud noise. The engine and the blades stopped, and when I looked under the mower I could see that something had come apart. It cost $353 to repair. Because I had neglected to maintain service on another part of the mower, my savings were gone. There was no excuse for my lack of attention.

I experienced some significant anger (resentment) during this process. I had some **blocked goals**. **I felt guilty**. I had **not honored my own morals and values** of keeping things properly serviced. **I felt some injustice** because I should have known better. I **felt threatened** as I realized I could have been injured when it broke down. As I began to process my anger, I knew only two choices were safe and pleasing to God. My anger had to be used to bring about a good change or it had to be dropped. The truth wasn't that I had too many pieces of equipment to maintain, or that I didn't have time to maintain them. I had simply allowed maintaining equipment to slip down my priority list. I decided to use the anger associated with this unnecessary costly situation to motivate me to make changes so it would not happen again.

These examples illustrate how we live in a fallen world. Daily we experience situations that produce the normal God-given emotion of anger (resentment). The question is not whether we will experience anger (resentment) today, but whether we will recognize, take ownership and process it in a way that pleases God.

14 Truths vs. 14 Myths About Anger

Let's compare the truth about anger (resentment) versus what I heard and learned growing up.

1. **Anger is a normal God-given emotion. Truth!**
   My childhood had shown me that often the adults in my life couldn't see their anger or they justified it; yet they always saw my anger and told me it wasn't appropriate or justified.

2. **Anger is a natural and normal response to many situations. Truth!**
   As I grew up, I had heard, "You shouldn't feel that way." "What is the matter with you?" "You better change your attitude and get that look off of your face."

3. **Anger is typically fueled or energized by hurt, frustration or fear. Truth!**
   I had heard, "You are all right." "Calm down and get over it!" "You shouldn't be afraid."

4. **Anger is often experienced during the forgiveness process. Truth!**
   This is what I heard growing up. "You have to forgive

25

and forget." "Let me remind you of what you have done."

5. **Anger does not automatically go away with time. Truth!**

   I had heard, "Put the past in the past!" "You ought to be grateful and happy."

6. **Anger builds unless it is processed to closure. Truth!**

   I had heard, "What is wrong with you?" "Why do you act like that when something happens?" "You can't get angry about everything that doesn't go your way."

7. **Anger can include a false sense of control and power. Truth!**

   I had heard, "You are being selfish." "You are being stubborn." Later I learned when we feel overwhelmed we instinctively try to move away from powerlessness.

8. **Anger is often misunderstood. Truth!**

   I had heard, "Tell me why you are upset." My reply was, "I don't know." "Yes, you do. Now tell me why you are mad."

9. **Anger is often mislabeled. Truth!**

   I had heard, "You're just having a pity party and feeling sorry for yourself." "Oh, he is just being quiet today."

10. **Anger, if chronic, is hazardous to our health. Truth!**

    I had heard, "I don't know why your stomach (or head) hurts and you stay sick all the time."

11. **Anger leads to emotional exhaustion and depression. Truth!**

    I had heard, "Why are you so tired all the time?" "Why do you look sad? You ought to be happy and have lots of energy."

12. Anger typically begins as resentment. Truth!
I had heard, "Why do you have a chip on your shoulder all the time?" "That is nothing to be upset over."

13. Anger can become rage. Truth!
I had heard, "Why do you overreact to everything? You're just not right (normal) when you get mad."

14. Anger requires God's help to restore peace, security and proper perspective. Truth!
I had heard, "Other people deal with things. You can too."

Oh, how I wish I had asked God for help before I was 32 years old! When I asked God for help, He began to teach me how to deal with life on His terms, using His resources. He began to change me into a safe person. I started:

- Learning and applying Biblical truth about emotions, especially anger management skills
- Taking ownership of my past and present condition rather than living in denial
- Recognizing the options God was offering for the future
- Stopping my attempts to figure out and fix everything on my own power
- Forgiving others and myself
- Grieving what was lost in a Godly manner
- Yielding to God's timing
- Embracing God's desire and ability to heal
- Finding my place in God's Kingdom and serving Him
- Learning to live by faith

Through this process God began to put the Fruit of the Spirit (love, joy, peace, patience, kindness, goodness, gentleness, faithfulness and self-control) and His perspective into my life.

We have five basic choices in managing the emotion of anger.

- **Suppression (worldly)** – the conscious intentional exclusion from consciousness of a thought or feeling. This choice stops healthy processing. It also contributes to a toxic level of internalized anger.

- **Aggression (worldly)** – any offensive action, assault or attack. This choice seeks to hurt others openly and to exact revenge.

- **Passive Aggression (worldly)** – expression of negative emotions in passive, indirect ways such as manipulation or noncooperation. This choice pretends to be ok, but seeks revenge covertly rather than openly. If we choose any of these (suppression, aggression, passive aggression) we are attempting to process our anger without God's help. It won't work.

- **Assertive to bring about good change (Godly)** – faith-led effort to protect others. This choice has phenomenal potential to use suffering and anger so others can be protected against similar suffering and anger. Mothers Against Drunk Driving (MADD) is an example of using anger from a loss to bring about social change to protect others in the future.

- **Drop it (Godly)** – release desire to understand or get even. This choice is challenging because it forces us to trust God and rely on faith. It can be the most liberating.

If we choose either of these (assertive to bring about good change or drop it) we are obeying God's command: "In your anger do not sin." (Ephesians 4:26) This allows God to direct our response and the processing of the anger.

This diagram illustrates the five choices. Which one is most common for you?

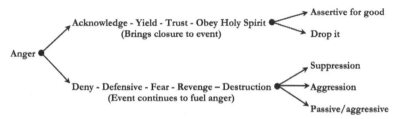

God has provided clear instructions and a timeline for processing anger

Consider the following Scripture. It holds some keys for how we can handle anger in the way that God instructs us.

"In your anger do not sin. Do not let the sun go down while you are still angry, and do not give the devil a foothold." (Ephesians 4:26-27)

Now, let's take the verses apart and examine them:

"In your anger do not sin."

God does not tell us to never experience anger. He tells us not to sin through the expression of our anger. Only by faith can we process our anger. If we express anger apart from faith, we sin. Romans 14:23b says, ". . . and everything that does not come from faith is sin."

"Do not let the sun go down while you are still angry. . ."

I cannot keep the sun from going down. I can, with God's help, be aware of and process my anger as I go through the day.

"Get rid of all bitterness, rage and anger, brawling and slander, along with every form of malice." (Ephesians 4:31) **"...and do not give the devil a foothold." (Eph. 4:27)**

Spiritual footholds almost always come about as a result of sin. The devil knows how important faith and forgiveness are to God. He also knows that our sin grieves the Holy Spirit of God (Ephesians 4:30). When the Holy Spirit is grieved, He withholds the Fruit of the Spirit. The Fruit of the Spirit are love, joy, peace, patience, kindness, goodness, faithfulness, gentleness and self-control. (Galatians 5:22-23) This allows the devil, through our sinful nature, to produce the fruit of the flesh, which includes sexual immorality, impurity, debauchery, idolatry, witchcraft, hatred, discord, jealousy, fits of rage, selfish ambition, dissensions, factions, envy, drunkenness, orgies and the like. (Galatians 5:19-21) Today we might also include pride, a legalistic attitude, a judgmental mindset, impure thoughts, jealousy, a critical spirit, guilt, worry, fear, discouragement, impatience and aimlessness.

When the devil gains a spiritual foothold, distress – which can be spiritual, mental, emotional or physical – usually occurs. This distress can lead to depression, anxiety, bitterness, worry or irrational thoughts. When our emotional pain increases, so does the perceived need and extreme desire to change the way we feel. Sometimes we try to change the way we feel by manipulating people or circumstances. Sometimes we change the way we feel through self-medicating. Self-medication can be through drugs, pornography, gambling, alcohol or overeating. It is an attempt to escape, hide from, numb out to, or feel something other than the pain.

King David allowed a foothold when he did not forgive Shimeli, son of Gera (2 Samuel 16:5-12; 19:18-23; 1 Kings 2:8-9; 2:29-34) and Joab, son of Zeruiah (1 Kings 1:7; 2 Samuel 3:26-39; 1 Kings 2:5-6). David knew he was about to die so he ordered Solomon to kill Joab, son of Zeruiah and

Shimeli, son of Gera. With this order King David, through Solomon, got revenge for what these men had done.

Do you try to process your anger independently of God? Do you monitor your level of anger daily? Have you given the devil a foothold by continuing to live in sin? Have you passed to another person or generation, as David did to Solomon, your unfinished business? Would you rather live in the fruit of the flesh or the Fruit of the Holy Spirit of God?

A little poetry, if you please.

Those who study people have said it is true.
There are five situations that bring anger to you.
Some people believe a number of notions,
but anger is a God-given emotion.
When we feel threatened it is anger that motivates you,
to get out of the way without having to think what to do.
It is called the emotion of self-preservation.
It is a problem if without a justifiable situation.
Be careful when feeling guilty, which way you turn.
Some choices lead to tough lessons we have to learn.
The solution is not in acts of aggression,
but often in a simple heartfelt confession.
Injustice reminds us that life is not fair.
The problem is that too often we dare
to take matters into our own hands,
reacting to what is not right in this fallen land.
Blocked goals are such a cause of frustration.
Most times it is more than mild irritation.
I have my list and I'm working my plan.
My life won't cooperate I don't understand.
Morals and values are close to the heart.
When we don't honor them we aren't being smart.
If we want to avoid being in a fight,
we must remember people believe their perspective is right.

What practical steps helped me forgive
and manage my anger?

- Openly recognize the wrong to be wrong.
- Recognize that your anger is not only normal, it is necessary.
- Realize that ongoing bitterness will ultimately hurt you.
- Evaluate and make changes to boundaries as needed.
- Don't let this be about inferiority or superiority.
- Resist the temptation to judge. That is God's job.
- Allow yourself time and energy to grieve the loss.
- If necessary to stop the destruction, confront the offending person.
- Let go of the illusion of control. Focus on healing emotionally.
- Realize to become like Jesus, we must choose to forgive.
- Remember we all have sinned and need to be forgiven.
- Allow God to use your journey of faith to encourage other hurting people.

Our choices always include consequences. In the next chapter, I'll share some of my excuses for not forgiving and the consequences of my choices.

Chapter 3

What were my excuses for not forgiving?
What were the consequences?

Even after I became a Christian, I realized I lacked the peace that God wanted me to have. And even after I realized my anger was rooted in my inability to forgive those who had hurt me, I still found myself struggling.

I came to understand that I believed I had a right to withhold forgiveness. I believed that my hurt and my pain was worse than anyone else's. Because of that belief, I gave myself excuses for not forgiving. And I've seen those excuses surface in hundreds of people I've counseled. Person after person would come to me with their troubles and, even when they saw that their anger and anxiety was caused by unforgiveness, they felt they had an excuse for it.

What were my excuses for not forgiving?

"In the Bible it says you have to forgive seventy times seven. I want you all to know, I'm keeping a chart." Hillary

Rodham Clinton said, maybe half-jokingly.

Men, typically, trust their reasoning. "If it doesn't make sense to me, I won't agree."

Women, typically, trust their emotions. "If I don't feel it in my heart, then I can't be sure."

That is not to say that men don't have and trust emotions or that women do not have reasoning, but rather that **it is natural for us to either trust our reasoning or our emotions.** In our natural way of thinking, we believe we can find it in ourselves to deal with the psychic debt that's owed to us by those who have offended us.

Remember: while forgiveness may not make us right with the offender, it does make us right with God. Forgiveness may not change the relationship with the offender, but it does change our relationship with God.

However, at this point in my life, I had not realized that the journey of forgiveness was one of surrendering to His guidance, in faith. I was still trying to figure it out myself. When I couldn't, I came up with excuse after excuse for why I simply could not forgive.

Truth questions related to excuses:

Thankfully, the Lord did not allow me to keep living a life full of fear and anger by hiding behind excuses. He began to show me His truth, through His Word, about my excuses. Following are some of the questions I had and the truths about my excuses for not forgiving.

Is there a difference between recovery or healing and forgiving?

Yes. Forgiving disarms the painful experience. It does not heal, but rather provides some stability and brings the season of destruction to a close. It is possible to forgive, but never

34

be as we were before we were hurt. It is possible to be healed and learn new and better skills. God can take the bad thing that happened and use it for good. This does not mean that what happened is good, but rather it means that God is capable of using our suffering to facilitate His work in our lives. (Hebrews 2:10)

Shouldn't I expect the scales to be balanced and justice to be served?

We often want to dictate the consequences for the offender. 1 Cor. 4:3-5 states that God alone will judge each person, at the appointed time. God has not given us, as individuals, the final authority to determine guilt, innocence, or appropriate consequences for any person, even ourselves. Because we are created in the image and likeness of God, we have sensitivity to injustice. To be clear, we want mercy and grace for ourselves, but often we want justice for the person who caused our hurt or disappointment. We would do well to remember that we who are living have yet to experience God's final judgment. When we look at the price God paid to offer us forgiveness, we can be assured that the righteousness of God will successfully complete the process of evil being punished.

If we forgive, does that means the other person is no longer held accountable?

No. In the judicial systems of government a person who commits a crime goes through a process. Typically, they will appear before a judge. The judge will require a security deposit, bail or bond, to be sure the person returns at the appointed time to enter a plea. Even after they enter a plea, the final judgment has not been determined.

In the same way God determines the day and time that we will stand before Him.

If we forgive, does that imply that the offender is "off the hook?"

No. God's Word says in Romans 12:19 that "it is mine to repay. I will avenge." Often as we watch the judicial system function we wonder why things don't move faster. (Psalm 73:3-20) Even if someone has pleaded guilty, often their consequences such as fines, jail time and probation, are not known until a final hearing (sentencing) before the judge.

What if the offense was too great?

We might think, "Surely, God doesn't expect me to forgive now. My life has been changed by what happened and this is going to take time. I need to be sure justice is served." But would God's Spirit ever lead us to postpone forgiving? No. When God gives us faith, it is always in the right proportion. (Philippians. 4:19) He knows what has happened, and He knows what we need in order to trust Him with the debt owed to us. God has made available to us enough faith to trust His provision for our forgiveness, which was Jesus' death on a cross. The sins we commit against God require our death. (Romans 6:23) If our sin has the value of life or death to God and He has forgiven us, can anyone commit a sin against us that is greater than the sin for which God has forgiven us?

Doesn't the other person have to accept the forgiveness for it to be effective?

No. It is common for people to forgive someone who is already dead. We can certainly turn the debt owed us over to God, which is the process of forgiveness, but we can't communicate with someone who is dead. In many situations it is not safe or appropriate for the offender to be in the presence of the offended. If the offender blames the offended, refuses to accept forgiveness, or claims innocence, further damage will occur.

Don't we have to feel in our heart that we forgive, for it to be real?

No. We will not *feel* our way to forgiveness. It is an act of faith, in obedience to God. It takes nothing more than faith and requires nothing less than faith.

Emotions are like gauges on the dashboard of a vehicle. Gauges give us a reading, or information, about what is happening somewhere else. For example, a fuel gauge on the dash doesn't smell or feel like gasoline, but provides information. In the same way our emotions tell us what is going on inside.

That is not to say we shouldn't have feelings. However, we should put our faith first over our feelings. We should not allow our emotions to have more power than the truth of God's Word.

If we are not the offended person, are we not being disloyal to the offended person when we forgive the offender?

No. This is not about loyalty, choosing sides or judging. It is about participating in God's process of restoring hope, healing and giving direction.

For example, I know the divorce of my parents deeply wounded both of them. I needed to forgive both parents for the impact of their divorce on my life. But I also needed to forgive them for the impact of their decisions upon each other.

It is not my responsibility to determine who was right or wrong. My best option is to forgive all parties involved. Unless I forgive, I will continue to be wounded. Often those who don't forgive find a common bond in their anger and hurt. But they will also participate in the ongoing hurt and anger. If I forgive and one parent doesn't, I can pray for them, comfort them and demonstrate the positive impact of having forgiven.

If I forgive my dad and mom it doesn't mean I am choosing sides or excusing what happened. If I forgive my mom and dad it doesn't mean that I am any closer to either parent. It does mean that I will restore my relationship with God.

Victim questions related to excuses:

I realized I felt victimized by the wrongs committed against me. I could find no answers inside me or in my experience growing up (and into adulthood) that gave me the peace I craved. And the act of forgiveness made me feel more of a victim. Eventually, the Lord began to teach me the truths and myths about being a victim.

Doesn't it rob of us our personal power if we "just" forgive?

Not true. Victims often feel powerless. Instinctively we move away from powerlessness to avoid feeling vulnerable. One of the effects of anger is it causes us to feel like we have more power. But this feeling often leads to decisions we later regret. It takes much more courage to forgive, and to release the power of the anger, than to continue justifying our anger.

Don't our questions deserve to be answered?

Not true. Evil and sin never make sense. If we require everything to make sense before we forgive, we will remain in bondage. The common questions of "why" and "how could they" have no answer that will satisfy or justify. Philippians 4:19 teaches that God meets all our needs. That includes our need for knowledge. Faith is the priority, not satisfying answers. God has provided the faith we need to trust Him with what we know and with what we don't know. It is not our responsibility to analyze. God doesn't ask us to figure it out, but to trust Him enough to respond in faith.

If we forgive, does that imply we excuse their behavior?

No. We cannot make this about winning or losing. Regardless of how others respond it is essential that we make a faith-based decision. Romans 14:23b says "and everything that does not come from faith is sin."

If we forgive, does that mean we have to get over it or forget what happened?

No. There is a difference between forgiving and healing. Forgiveness allows the healing process to begin. For each person the journey to healing is unique. The Holy Spirit knows us better than we know ourselves. He will faithfully lead us to healing and resolution. He alone knows the challenges we face in trusting people.

If we forgive, do we have to tell them that we have forgiven them?

No. When we forgive another person, it is first and foremost between us and God. Once that process is completed, God leads us to the next step of faith.

If we forgive, should we insist on being reconciled to the offender?

No. If the person does not accept responsibility and is not repentant, then the offender is not a safe person. God does not lead His children into destruction nor does He require His children to continue to live in destruction.

If we forgive, do we have to be restored to them in relationship?

No. It depends upon the situation as to whether the relationship is terminated.

What if the person won't accept responsibility for their actions?

It is not our responsibility to force people to accept responsibility for their actions. It is our job to respond in faith and to trust God with all the other details and people.

What if the person isn't truly sorry about what happened?

We can forgive regardless of whether or not the person is sorry. Our forgiveness is not limited to their response to the situation. Forgiveness is never for the offender, it is always for the offended. In other words, we don't forgive for the benefit of the offender. We forgive because God commanded us to forgive.

What if the person did not ask for forgiveness?

Many times it is our desire to hear the person ask for forgiveness. However, we can't let a lack of action by the other person prevent us from doing what God has commanded us to do, which is to forgive.

What if it happened more than once and deliberately?

Just because we forgive, it does not mean that we allow ourselves to be hurt again. The offender may never accept responsibility, repent or stop being destructive. It is still our responsibility to forgive. But it is also our responsibility to not allow ourselves to be hurt again.

Shouldn't the people who hurt me have to make it right with me?

If we forgive them, then we turn the debt they owe us over to God. It is important that we realize that for some hurts there is no way to make it right. While a court of law could require restitution, on our own it isn't likely that we would agree on fair restitution.

Offender questions related to excuses:

At the same time I was learning how to forgive, I realized I needed to ask forgiveness of others. Sadly, I had concentrated so much on how I had been wronged but very little on how I'd wronged others. You might have some of the questions I had about how to ask for forgiveness.

Should I meet with the person to ask for forgiveness?

Wise counsel should influence this decision. If hearing the voice or being in the presence of the offender would be detrimental to healing and recovery, choose another method. Written communication has several advantages. It allows the offender the opportunity to ask forgiveness without the emotional intensity of a face-to-face conversation. Also, this can be therapeutic. It allows the offended to receive the forgiveness request without any perceived threat from being in the presence of the person who hurt them. This method also removes any pressure to answer immediately.

What about my problems that caused me to wrong someone?

Although angry and wounded people typically are the ones who wound others, there is no excuse for harming another person. Begin by asking God to forgive you. Then forgive yourself. Then forgive others. These are foundational steps in reducing the destruction in your life and through your life. Find a seasoned, wise Biblical counselor to speak truth into your life and walk with you through your journey of recovery. Learn to utilize the hope, skills and freedom that only God can offer to you. Make it your goal to allow God to change you so you can become a safe person.

Don't they have to forgive me?

Just because someone forgives you, it doesn't automatically mean that God will extend the relationship. While it is true that God wants you to be forgiven by the offended, you cannot use that as manipulative leverage to influence the other person.

Can I ever forgive myself?

Yes. While the enemy of our soul wants us to live in guilt, God wants us to experience the hope and healing of being forgiven. It is important to remember that God's grace is available and accepted by faith. It is also through faith that we forgive ourselves. If we have asked God to forgive us, according to His Word, we are forgiven. Since we do not have the authority to overrule God's verdict, we either accept it by faith or we reject it. When we reject the truth of our forgiveness, we will live in false guilt. False guilt occurs when we are forgiven by God, but continue to live as if we are guilty.

Is it true God will forgive me?

Yes. According to God's Word, if we confess our sins and ask for forgiveness, He will forgive us. It is important to remember that we do not have to feel forgiven to be forgiven. Our forgiveness does not have to make sense to us for us to be forgiven.

What if what I did is being blown out of proportion?

To ask forgiveness is to admit wrongdoing. It does not mean that we necessarily agree with the extent of the damage, the motivation or the consequences. We ask to be forgiven because God has commanded us to ask to be forgiven.

"Therefore, if you are offering your gift at the altar and there remember that your brother has something against you, leave your gift there in front of the altar. First go and be reconciled to your brother; then come and offer your gift." (Matthew 5:23)

Shouldn't life be fair?

Life was fair when God created the heavens and the earth. There was no sin; therefore there were no consequences of sin. There was no fear, shame or guilt. This was God's original design for mankind. Because we live in a season between the Garden of Eden and Paradise, and because sin has touched our lives, fairness is not our best option. If life were fair, justice would be served immediately, and the penalty of our sin would have been incurred after our first sin. The Bible clearly teaches that the penalty for sin is death. God offers something better than fair. He offers grace, which is unmerited favor. In other words, we don't have to experience the just payment for our sin.

Three truths provide hope, stability and courage while living in a fallen world. One, I don't expect life to be fair. Two, I know that God is faithful. Three, He knows what He is doing and can be trusted.

"Forgiveness has nothing to do with absolving a criminal of his crime. It has everything to do with relieving oneself of the burden of being a victim—letting go of the pain and transforming oneself from victim to survivor." C.R. Strahan

Consequences of not forgiving:

Through the years, I saw how my unforgiveness had affected me negatively. And I've seen these consequences in so many others who have traced their problems back to the root of unforgiveness. As I realized how God planned to get rid of these negatives through the action of forgiveness, I gained more incentive to rid myself of the excuses I had collected. Some of the consequences of not forgiving:

- Stress – caused by fear, anger and bitterness
- Re-injury – caused by repeatedly reliving the painful events
- Loss of love – caused by walls of protection
- Isolation – caused by fear of being hurt
- Confusion – caused by trying to understand "why"
- Negativity – caused by discouragement
- Estrangement – caused by others avoiding my resentment and harshness
- Exhaustion – caused by lack of rest
- Depression - caused by emotional exhaustion
- Jealousy – caused by envy of others
- Pride – caused by rebellion and selfishness
- Anger – caused by desire for revenge and hatred
- Often sick – caused by compromised immune system
- Discontentment – caused by greed

Does the Bible say there are consequences of me not forgiving? YES!

I had read the following story of Jesus many times before. One day, however, it sunk in: God's assurance to me that I'd been forgiven by Him was connected proportionately to my active forgiveness of others who had wronged me.

"Then Peter came to Jesus and asked, 'Lord, how many times shall I forgive my brother when he sins against me? Up to seven times?' Jesus answered, 'I tell you, not seven times, but seventy-seven times.

"Therefore, the kingdom of heaven is like a king who wanted to settle accounts with his servants. As he began the settlement, a man who owed him ten thousand talents was brought to him. Since he was not able to pay, the master ordered that he and his wife and his children and all that he had be sold to repay the debt.

"The servant fell on his knees before him. 'Be patient with me,' he begged, 'and I will pay back everything.' The servant's master took pity on him, canceled the debt and let him go."

"But when that servant went out, he found one of his fellow servants who owed him a hundred denarii. He grabbed him and began to choke him. 'Pay back what you owe me!' he demanded. The servant fell to his knees and begged him, 'Be patient with me, and I will pay you back.'

"But he refused. Instead, he went off and had the man thrown into prison until he could pay the debt. When the other servants saw what had happened, they were greatly distressed and went and told their master everything that had happened."

"Then the master called the servant in. 'You wicked servant,' he said, 'I canceled all that debt of yours because you begged me to. Shouldn't you have had mercy on your fellow servant just as I had on you?' In anger his master turned him over to the jailers to be tortured, until he should pay back all he owed."

"'This is how my heavenly Father will treat each of you unless you forgive your brother from your heart.'" (Matthew 18:21-35)

According to this Scripture, if I do not forgive I will be "turned over to the jailers to be tortured." But why does God include such details in this story? He is showing us the difference between how much He has forgiven us and how much he requires us to forgive others.

If we ask God to forgive us, then we identify with the servant who owed ten thousand talents. You may be wondering just how many United States dollars equal 10,000 talents? I'm glad you asked. **10,000 talents = 150,000 years' wages**

This is how that number is calculated:

- 1 talent = 60 minas
- 1 mina = 3 months' wages
- 1 talent = 60 x (3 months' wages) = 180 months' wages
- 1 talent = 180 months' wages / 12 months in a year = 15 years' wages
- 1 talent = 15 years' wages
- 10,000 talents = 150,000 years' wages

If a yearly wage is $16,640 (about 40 hours per week at $8.00 per hour), then 150,000 years' wages = $2,496,000,000 (2 billion, 496 million US dollars)

When we ask God to forgive us, we owed Him approximately $2,496,000,000. That is 2 billion, 496 million dollars, which equals 10,000 talents. He showed mercy and forgave (canceled) our debt. Actually he collected on our debt when Jesus was on the cross paying for our sins!

How much did the other servant owe, in comparison? I'm glad you asked.

- 1 denarii = 1 days' wages (about $64 in US dollars)
- 100 denarii = approximately $6,400. That is 6,400 hundred dollars.

When God commands us to forgive others, the debt they owe is always much smaller than the debt we owed God, which He forgave.

A little poetry, if you please.

I met a woman the other day.
At first she didn't have much to say.
I listened, smiled and tried to connect.
What happened next I didn't expect.
Her teeth were clinched and her face was flushed.
I knew this process could not be rushed.
The hurt was deep, her pain was real.
I knew the only hope was for God to heal.
When I mentioned His name, she quickly drew back.
If her questions were all written they would have made quite a stack.
With everything in me I wanted to help her move along.
I thought I'd mention words from a song.
Then it became very clear
that what I had to say she didn't want to hear.
I thought that maybe God would calm her soul through prayer.
But when I asked she said, "Don't you dare."
"I stopped talking to Him some time back,
because where was He when my world turned black?"
I said, "I don't have an answer that will make this right,
but if I don't talk to God when I lay my head down tonight,
I'll be one step closer to where I used to be
and that won't be good for anyone, especially me."

Chapter 4

Where did I learn my definition of forgiveness? Was it different from God's?

Several years ago, I began to experience a ringing sound in my ears. Because of the loud machine shops I had worked in for many years, and the loud music I had listened to when I was younger, the ringing did not surprise me. It was driving me crazy, however, because the noise kept changing.

I went to the doctor, was examined and tested. He told me that there was no structural problem that could be repaired. He wanted me to take a medication and to monitor which ear was ringing at what time of day and in what setting.

A few weeks later, I was shopping in Wal-Mart. It seemed the ringing had changed that day and so I was really focused on it. As I was standing in the checkout line, the cashier looked at me and said, "Sir, you are ringing." I looked at her in shock and asked, "Can you hear this ringing in my ears?" She looked at me as if I had lost my mind, pointed to my cell phone and said, "It is your cell phone!" Now both of us heard a ringing sound. But we were not talking about the same thing.

We often talk about forgiveness, but our definition may be very different than God's definition.

Satan knows God is very sensitive about how we, as His children, process forgiveness. That is why Satan will invest so much effort into our getting stuck in the process. A strategy of Satan is to distort God's definition of forgiveness and to convince us that we are justified in not forgiving. Satan knows how much the righteousness of God demanded in order for the mercy and grace of God to be released, on our behalf.

Some people gain a clear understanding of forgiveness easier than others. For me, a clear understanding required that I know what forgiveness was *not*.

Nine things that are not forgiveness:

1. Forgiveness does not mean that we pretend nothing happened when we were offended. That is lying about it. An offense occurred. While God's Word says that He puts our sins as far as the east is from the west and remembers them no more, He does not tell us we have to forget to forgive. As a matter of fact, if the person is still unsafe, it is best we do remember it and avoid putting ourselves in harm's way.

2. Forgiveness does not mean that the offense doesn't matter. What happened does matter, and if I dismiss it and act like it doesn't matter, the resentment does not go away.

3. Forgiveness does not mean that we forget. God does not call or lead His children to destruction. So, to remember

the event and the offender person is a part of limiting the destruction in the future.

4. Forgiveness does not mean that we stop hurting automatically. The grief process and healing from relational wounds is painful and challenging. It requires courage and commitment to be healed. After I forgave my dad, it took me two or three years to be able to sit in church on Father's Day. The wounds were just too deep. When I would look around and see three generations of family sitting together and hear the message about good, godly fathers, I became overwhelmed. Grieving my losses could not be successfully completed until I forgave. By the grace of God, I actually preached on Fathers' Day about 10 or 11 years after I forgave my dad. When the invitation began, the altar was full. A powerful component of my healing took place that day as I witnessed God using my story in a powerful way.

5. Forgiveness does not always mean we understand why someone hurt us. If we are trying to do what is right, it will never make sense as to why someone would hurt us. Many times we are caught up in the circumstances of others' choices as the consequences overflow. For example, children can be hurt by the way their parents treat each other. The parents may be directing the hurt to each other, but the children are exposed to the situation.

6. Forgiveness does not mean that we are okay with what happened. When we forgive we are not saying that we approve of what happened because we now understand. We may never be okay with what happened because wrong is always wrong. Wrong is never right. We trust God, however, to bring His good results out of bad events and situations.

7. Forgiveness does not mean that the offender deserves to be forgiven. It is God's job to decide who receives forgiveness. If we have been forgiven by God it is always a gift of grace. Many times the wrong cannot be undone or made right. Many times there is no going back to the way things were before the injury occurred.

8. Forgiveness does not always mean that we are reconciled to that person. Forgiveness reconciles us to God, not to the other person. What God tells us to do with the relationship is another step of faith apart from the forgiveness process. This is especially true if the other person does not acknowledge or take ownership of what happened.

9. Forgiveness does not mean that we are restored relationally to the offender. The offense may close the door to continued relationship with that person. For example, if the other person has no interest in the relationship, we certainly cannot be restored to them. God determines the seasons of our lives as well as those who will be a part of that season. In other words, just because someone has been a part of my life in the past, it doesn't automatically mean they will be part of my life in the future.

The Right Sources Gives the Right Information

Like many people in our family, my son loved to go fishing – if it wasn't too hot and the fish were biting. One day when he was seven, we were on our way home after another hot, fishless trip when I heard him say these words: "Dad, I don't think you are smart enough to catch a fish." Even though it has been more than thirty years since that happened, I can remember feeling ashamed, angry and discouraged. I brooded on that statement for a few days.

I told one of my workers at the shop what had happened. He was passionate about fishing and had even fished professionally for a few years. He told me to go where a small stream flowed into the river. He said to go right before dark, just put a worm on the line and don't use a float. Then he smiled and said to take two poles because my son would catch fish faster than I could take them off and put new bait back on.

That afternoon I was excited to prove myself to my son. I stopped at the bait shop and hurried home. He wasn't going. Finally I talked him into giving me one more chance. I carefully followed the instructions I had been given. We caught 21 fish in 45 minutes!

When I went to the right source for information, good results followed.

That's how God's Word works to give us good results in our lives. Consider the following passages:

"Blessed is the man who does not walk in step with the wicked or stand in the way that sinners take or sit in the company of mockers, but whose delight is in the law of the Lord, and who meditates on his law day and night. That person is like a tree planted by streams of water, which yields its fruit in season and whose leaf does not wither-- whatever they do prospers." (Psalm 1:1-3)

"Do not conform any longer to the pattern of this world, but be transformed by the renewing of your mind." (Romans 12:2)

"For though we live in the world, we do not wage war as the world does. The weapons we fight with are not the weapons of the world. On the contrary, they have divine power to demolish strongholds. We demolish arguments and every pretension that sets itself up against the knowledge of

God, and we take captive every thought to make it obedient to Christ." (2 Corinthians 10:3-5)

God's Definition of Forgiveness

According to God's Word, forgiveness means that I turn the debt owed to me over to God to collect on. It is an act of faith between God and me. I will agree with God and obey or I will refuse to agree with God and live in sin.

As God continued to work in my life, I became more sensitive to God's Word and the leading of the Holy Spirit. While some things had changed for the better, my thought life stunk! I asked God to help me think about what I was thinking about. I knew the thoughts in my head were not pleasing to God but they continued. You see, I brought with me into the Kingdom of God a toxic waste dump located between my ears. Just because God had forgiven me and changed my life, it didn't mean that my brain was automatically cleaned up or images from the past erased. And my emotions were still not functioning correctly. It seemed my emotions, especially anger, still had too much power in my life. It wasn't until later that I learned that <u>thoughts produce feelings, and that thoughts and feelings influence action</u>.

I searched the Bible for an answer to the question, "Where do thoughts come from?" While reading and meditating on Matthew Chapter 16, Jesus' conversation with His disciples caught my attention. Verse 17 clearly says that the Holy Spirit put thoughts in Simon's, son of Jonah (Peter), mind. "… for this was not revealed to you by man, but by my Father in heaven." So, some thoughts are put into my mind by the Holy Spirit. But as I continued, verse 23a seemed to say that Satan was putting thoughts into Peter's mind. "Jesus turned and said to Peter, 'Get behind me Satan!'" It is as if

Jesus is telling Satan that he knows who he is and what he is doing. Jesus was not confused about who he was talking to. So, my observation is that some thoughts were put into Peter's mind by Satan. So, some thoughts are put into my mind by Satan. Jesus continued the verse, now talking to Peter, "You are a stumbling block to me; you do not have in mind the things of God, but the things of men." It is my observation that verse 23b says people can and do put thoughts into my mind. This is illustrated below.

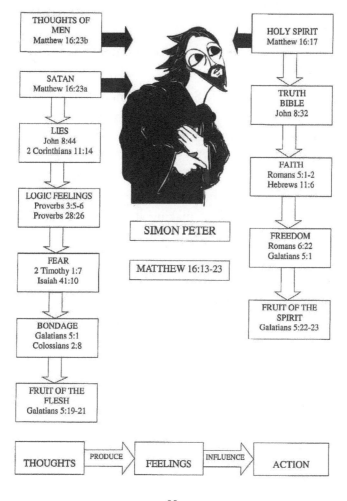

THOUGHTS OF MEN
Matthew 16:23b

HOLY SPIRIT
Matthew 16:17

SATAN
Matthew 16:23a

TRUTH
BIBLE
John 8:32

LIES
John 8:44
2 Corinthians 11:14

FAITH
Romans 5:1-2
Hebrews 11:6

LOGIC FEELINGS
Proverbs 3:5-6
Proverbs 28:26

SIMON PETER

FREEDOM
Romans 6:22
Galatians 5:1

FEAR
2 Timothy 1:7
Isaiah 41:10

MATTHEW 16:13-23

BONDAGE
Galatians 5:1
Colossians 2:8

FRUIT OF THE SPIRIT
Galatians 5:22-23

FRUIT OF THE FLESH
Galatians 5:19-21

THOUGHTS → PRODUCE → FEELINGS → INFLUENCE → ACTION

While there are three sources thoughts come from, there are only two categories. Either the Holy Spirit is putting thoughts into my mind or they are coming from somewhere else. Clearly, only one category was blessed by Jesus. The other was confronted and rebuked.

Why is this so important? Let me repeat: Thoughts produce feelings. Thoughts and feelings influence action. If I want my thought life, emotions and actions to be pleasing to God, I have to ask myself, "Where did that thought come from? Would God's Holy Spirit put that thought in my mind?"

What do we know about these opposing sources of thoughts?

● We know that the Holy Spirit would never put a thought in our mind that does not line up with the truth of God's Word. (See previous illustration – right side.) "Then you will know the truth, and the truth will set you free." (John 8:32) "But when he, the Spirit of Truth, comes, he will guide you into all truth. He will bring glory to me by taking from what is mine and making it known to you." (John 16:13-14)

● We also know that the Holy Spirit is responsible for completing the good work He began in us by making us people of faith. "And without faith it is impossible to please God, because anyone who comes to him must believe he exists and that he rewards those who earnestly seek him." (Hebrews 11:6) "Being confident of this, that he who began a good work in you will carry it on to completion until the day of Christ Jesus." (Philippians 1:6b) We are told "to be conformed to the likeness of His Son." (Romans 8:29)

- This ongoing work of the Holy Spirit produces freedom. "But now you have been set free from sin." (Romans 6:22a) "It is for freedom that Christ has set us free." (Galatians 5:1a)

- The Holy Spirit wants to put the Fruit of the Spirit in us. "So I say, live by the Spirit, and you will not gratify the desires of the sinful nature." (Galatians 5:16) "But the fruit of the Spirit is love, joy, peace, patience, kindness, goodness, faithfulness, gentleness and self-control. Against such things there is no law." (Galatians 5:22-23) "Since we live by the Spirit, let us keep in step with the Spirit." (Galatians 5:25)

- Thoughts come into my mind that I know are not from the Holy Spirit. Satan deals in speculation and lies. These lies often include half a truth or a truth and a half. He is always using distortion to gain our attention and focus. Many times people will speak with confidence and try to influence, without questioning whether or not the Holy Spirit is leading them to speak.

"But I tell you that men will have to give account on the Day of Judgment for every careless word they have spoken." (Matthew 12:36) "You belong to your father, the devil, and you want to carry out your father's desires. He was a murderer from the beginning, not holding to the truth, for there is no truth in him. When he lies, he speaks his native language, for he is a liar and the father of all lies." (John 8:44) "For such men are false apostles, deceitful workmen, masquerading as apostles of Christ. And no wonder, for Satan himself masquerades as an angel of light. It is not surprising, then, if his servants masquerade as servants of righteousness. Their end will be what their actions deserve." (2 Corinthians 11:13-15)

- Just like he deceived Adam and Eve in the Garden, Satan wants us to depend on our logic and reasoning or our feelings to determine our course of action. Certainly we do not turn our brain off or pretend we don't have emotions, but we cannot allow what makes sense to us and our feelings to have more power than the truth of God's Word. (See illustration – left side.) "Trust in the Lord with all your heart and lean not on your own understanding; in all your ways acknowledge him, and he will make your paths straight. Do not be wise in your own eyes." (Proverbs 3:5-7) "He who trusts in himself is a fool, but he who walks in wisdom is kept safe." (Proverbs 28:26)

- While the Holy Spirit uses faith in God's character and God's Word, Satan's tool is to motivate us with fear. Fear has a proper place, such as when we are in danger. Satan uses fear to get us to take matters into our own hands. In the Garden, he convinced Adam and Eve that they should assess for themselves whether or not to eat from the fruit of the forbidden tree.

  "When the woman saw that the fruit of the tree was good for food and pleasing to the eye, and also desirable for gaining wisdom, she took some and ate it. She also gave some to her husband, who was with her, and he ate it." (Genesis 3:6)

- Satan often tries to convince us that God is withholding from us. Fear is a God-given emotion. More than 360 times God says in His Word, to His people, that we should not live in fear. That indicates it is both a common problem and God is persistent about addressing the problem.

  "For God did not give us a spirit of timidity (fear), but a spirit of power, of love and of self-discipline." (2 Timothy 1:7) "So do not fear, for I am with you; do not be dismayed, for I am your God. I will strengthen you and uphold you with my righteous right hand." (Isaiah 41:10)

"There is no fear in love. But perfect love drives out fear." (1 John 4:18)

- Satan wants to take God's people prisoners of war. He wants us to be in bondage with worry, guilt, a legalistic attitude, impure thoughts, jealousy, discouragement, a critical spirit, frustration and aimlessness. When God says we should not allow fear to control our lives, He knows that He is the only one who can deliver us from fear. "Do not let yourselves be burdened again by a yoke of slavery." (Galatians 5:1b) "See to it that no one takes you captive through hollow and deceptive philosophy, which depends on human tradition and the basic principles of this world rather than on Christ." (Colossians 2:8) "Or again, how can anyone enter a strong man's house and carry off his possessions unless he first ties up the strong man? Then he can rob his house." (Matthew 12:29)

- Satan wants us to be positioned so that we do not have the Fruit of the Spirit, but rather have the fruit of the flesh. He knows we will live in defeat, guilt, fear and shame. "The acts of the sinful nature are obvious: sexual immorality, impurity and debauchery; idolatry and witchcraft; hatred, discord, jealousy, fits of rage, selfish ambition, dissensions, factions and envy; drunkenness, orgies, and the like." (Galatians 5:19-21)

Let me repeat: Thoughts produce feelings....thoughts and feelings influence action. If I want my feelings to change and work properly, I have to think about what I am thinking about.

I remember my grandmother talking about my need to practice patience. I don't know if she practiced it, but she sure preached it to me! But when we look at Scripture, patience is not acquired through practice, but rather is one of the fruits of the Spirit God gives us as a gift, when we trust Him.

A little poetry, if you please.

Why do I trust my reasoning and emotions
Rather than Your Word with complete devotion
Living in a fallen world makes no sense
When I try to connect often I find a fence.
The devil loves to whisper in my ear
You have many reasons to fear
God can't be trusted he loves to say
Get what you can and do it today
He knows and uses the code to the sin nature
To keep me from experiencing God's favor,
I have to be careful to monitor my thought life.
To have any hope of experiencing less strife
I've allowed people, the devil and many situations
To rob me of peace and joy and leave me in frustration.
Help me please God to trust you and your Word today
Regardless of what makes sense, I feel or others say.

Chapter 5

Did forgiveness improve my quality of life?

For many years I lived my life through the emotion of anger. I not only disliked myself, I hated myself. And, even though I knew there were people who loved me, I felt it was because they had to, not because they knew and liked me. Even worse, even though I believed that God loved me, it was only because He had to. He certainly didn't like me.

As God led me to experience His grace through forgiveness, He also led me to forgive myself and others. One day God allowed me to realize I needed to get to know the person He made me to be. I had a lot of information about who I shouldn't be, but little about the person God created me to be. It was an amazing process to go from seeing myself and my life through an "anger filter" to seeing life from God's perspective. God took me through a process to understand and accept the truth that He made me exactly like He wanted to. Since God made me, who was I to critique His work?

It wasn't that God wanted me to be proud or self-righteous. God wanted me to rest in my soul about myself. Only by doing this was I trusting Him with my life. Only by doing this was I delivered from myself. Only by doing this was I available to worship and serve God.

Amazingly, I began to see the many positive results of forgiveness in my life. Following are 13 of those positives:

1. **I had less stress because forgiveness reduced fear, anger and bitterness.**

   If you had asked me "what are you afraid of?", I would have said nothing. But looking back I realize that the fear of failure and the fear of rejection were powerful forces in my life. This caused me to live at the fight-or-flight level constantly, which is very stressful.

2. **I began healing emotionally because I didn't have to relive the painful events.**

   The abundant life Jesus promised can only be experienced in the present moment. As I more fully trusted Him, He began to guard my heart and mind with peace. He allowed me to rest in my soul.

3. **I let my guard down and experienced more of the love available to me.**

   Being defensive and questioning everyone's motives was exhausting. Trying to make sure no one ripped me off or played me for a fool was no longer necessary.

4. **I felt less isolated because I didn't have to be afraid of anyone coming close emotionally.**

   Carrying the weight of the world around on my shoulders was exhausting. God began to change my priorities as I began to value the people in my life more than getting things done.

5. **I could live more in today because I didn't need to have my "why" questions answered.**

   It was such a blessed change when God convinced me I could trust Him with the unanswered questions. He gave me the faith to trust Him with what I knew and with what I didn't know.

6. **My attitude, about myself and about life, became more positive.**

   For many years I perceived myself through my bad choices and failures. As God began to change this, He allowed me to see His fingerprints along the way. What a relief it was to no longer need to prove anything to myself or anyone else!

7. **I no longer felt estranged and, therefore, became a safer person, emotionally. This allowed those who loved me to come closer.**

   When God saved me, He birthed me into a new family. This new family loved me and offered me a place to belong and serve. God allowed me to realize that I wasn't the only one who had made bad choices and failed.

8. **I had more energy.**

   Because I was no longer constantly living in the fight-or-flight mode, I slept better and wasn't tired when I awoke. I no longer had to make sense of my past, and I no longer had to worry about the future.

9. **I was able to see the good things in my life and was, therefore, more content.**

   While problems and frustrations didn't go away, the

way I processed them changed. Until God began to give me contentment, my focus was always on what I didn't have and what I needed to repair. God opened my eyes to see all He had given me and had done for me.

10. **My pride began to diminish, relieving me of the need to prove anything to myself or to others.**

After I got fired from the first machine shop I worked in, I spent the next 22 years pushing myself to not make a mistake that would get me fired again. I had to be the best tool maker wherever I worked. After God changed me, I realized that my employment was in God's hands. I could forgive myself and others. This allowed me to enjoy my skilled trade and focus on being available as a witness for Christ.

11. **I was less angry, less hateful, and less desirous of revenge.**

No amount of revenge can make right the offense of some wounds. What a difference it made when God allowed me to realize I didn't have to be angry anymore. For over thirty years I had allowed people and circumstances to rob me of the peace and joy of a relationship with God. God provided me with a choice.

12. **I was physically healthier because my immune system wasn't as stressed.**

Studies show that approximately 85% of treated illness is not directly related to disease. It is directly related to the impact of improperly managed stress. As I lost the stress of unforgiveness, I became healthier.

13. I found contentment and wasn't afraid I might miss something.

What a relief I began to experience as I "let go" of keeping track of who had offended me and why. As God showed me He could take care of those offenses, I gained His peace.

I look back and can see an amazing transformation in my life as I was delivered from greed and became willing to *give* in order to help those in need.

Whatever the situation, the first order of business is to forgive by faith so the destruction doesn't continue. Then healing can begin. When we forgive we are free to heal spiritually, mentally, emotionally and physically. Our stress level is reduced and our immune system has more resources available for restoring our health. We are not burning up and wasting so much energy with non-productive anger. Bitterness is an expensive emotional choice in terms of how it depletes our energy reserves.

This allows us to begin to put the past in God's care. It is very challenging to deal with today's business if I am also trying to deal with yesterday's business.

Overall, the practice of forgiving allows us to begin to use emotional energy in a productive way. Our relationships become safe, opening the paths to love and to be loved.

Let's say that God gives us $1.00 of emotional energy for each day. Before I experienced God's forgiveness, forgave myself and others, I would often burn up $.25 (25% of my emotional energy) before leaving for work. I might be annoyed over an insult from the day before, or from someone getting the last cup of coffee. Maybe my boss had lied to me again, or maybe I had made a mistake and I feared being chewed out.

If someone pulled out in front of my Harley on the way to work, there went another $.15 (15%) of my emotional energy. I was down to 60% before I had punched my time card to start a 12-hour shift in the machine shop.

As a supervisor, I tried to treat the skilled craftsmen with respect. But the shop owner believed he could get more work out of a person if they were mad at him. So he would intimidate. He could tear down more teamwork and respect in fifteen minutes than I could build in a week. Every time I saw him coming out of the office into the shop, the hair on the back of my neck would stand because I knew we would have words before he left the shop. There went the rest of my $.60 (60%) of emotional energy.

As I trusted God, received His forgiveness, and forgave myself and others, I realized I did not have to give away my emotional energy by asking questions only God could answer.

Freedom for me came as I understood three great truths:

1. Forgiveness allows us to let go of the "why" question. Whether or not I ever understand why something happened, I can still trust God with that question. God gives us the faith to trust him with what we do know and with what we don't know.

2. Forgiveness allows us to let go of the "how could they" question. When people do things that are out of character, it will never make sense.

3. Forgiveness allows me to become a safer person, both for myself and for others.

Section II

Getting Practical with Forgiveness

Every story has a beginning, a middle and an end.

So it is with my story of finding peace through forgiveness.

*It began with my acceptance, by faith, of forgiveness
by God, through Christ. It continued as He gave me, by faith,
the ability to forgive myself for the mess I had made
of my life. And it goes on, even today,
as I seek, by faith, to forgive others.*

You have your own story to live out.

You can have peace, by faith, through forgiveness.

Go ahead. Take that first step.

Let's take the first step on our journey.

Chapter 6

Where do we start?
How did forgiveness change my life?

It was April 17, 1987, and I remember the sun shining that morning. For the people who worked at the First Baptist Church in Columbia, Tennessee, I suppose it was just another Thursday. Inside my heart and mind, however, there was nothing but stormy weather.

I was desperately seeking peace in my life.

I had called the church earlier in the week to set up an appointment with the pastor. I was confused, nervous and I didn't trust people, especially anyone with more education than I had. But somehow I knew this preacher had peace in his life. I had heard him talk about it the previous Sunday when I had attended that service to see if peace was available to me.

After we were seated in his office, I told the preacher, "I need peace in my life and I don't care what it takes. I will do anything." He asked a few questions to get to know me better. I explained that I prayed the prayer, had been baptized and joined a church when I was young. Nothing really changed in my life at that time, so I just pretended to be a Christian. I thought that was what everybody else was doing. I continued pretending until I finished high school. Then, in anger I walked away from church.

For some reason, I knew I could tell him something I had believed for a long time, but had never said out loud. "I don't think God wants a relationship with me. I have messed up every relationship a man can mess up. I am a relationship failure."

The preacher leaned forward and said, "I can help you find peace." What a relief! Then he quoted Romans 5:8. "God demonstrated His love for us in this, while we were still sinners, Christ died for the ungodly." Then the preacher put it in terms I could understand. "Either God wants a relationship with you or He is a liar, Mike." I replied, "I don't know God, but I know He is not a liar." Continuing, he explained that when God created us, He didn't create us with the ability to run our own life. Jeremiah was praying and said, "I know, oh Lord, that a man's life is not his own; it is not within man to direct his own steps." (Jeremiah 10:23) I had been trying to run my life for 32 ½ years. It may have looked good on the outside, because we lived in a new house, had great jobs, had new vehicles and I had the nicest Harley Davidson motorcycle in town. On the inside, I was a mess. I was so tired of being angry and running from life. I didn't like being angry, but I didn't know how to not be angry.

I don't know what the preacher prayed that day. I do remember some of what I prayed. "God, you have run the world all these years without any trouble. I've tried to run my life my whole life. Since I've tried everything else I know to do, if you'll have it, Sir, I'm just going to give it to you. I ask you to forgive me and I surrender control to you."

I could not have told you – book, chapter and verse – what happened to me that day, because I knew very little about the Bible. I can tell you a tremendous weight came off me, replaced with peace that I had never experienced. While I was trying to understand what had happened I began to hear a voice. I looked at the other people in the room. They weren't talking. I thought either God is talking to me or I have gone crazy or maybe both! The voice kept saying, "It's going to be okay, Mike. You don't have to be angry anymore."

I had experienced the forgiveness of God. I had gone from being a lost person – separated by my sin from God – to becoming a born again child of God.

You can experience God's forgiveness!

If you have not yet experienced God's forgiveness, you can! <u>God wants to forgive you more than you want to be forgiven</u>. He has proven His desire for a relationship with you. God's Word is clear about the forgiveness process.

1. Agree with God about our problem (sin): "For all have sinned and fallen short of the glory of God." (Romans 3:23) The penalty of sin is death, separation from God and heaven. We will spend eternity in hell. "For the wages of sin is death." (Romans 6:23)

2. Agree with God's Word about the solution (Jesus): "For God so loved the world that he gave his one and only Son, that whoever believes in him shall not perish but have eternal life. For God did not send his Son into the world to condemn the world, but to save the world through him." (John 3:16-17) "But God

demonstrates His love for us in this: while we were still sinners, Christ died for us." (Romans 5:8) Because of His love for us, God sent Jesus to live a perfect life and to offer that perfect life through death on the cross. Jesus paid our sin debt!

3. Accept God's gift of forgiveness and salvation – on His terms. To receive Jesus' payment for our sins, we must believe in God, through the faith He provides, ask Him to save us by trusting Jesus as the only Savior and yielding control to Jesus as Lord. This is the surrender referred to in Jeremiah 10:23. Romans 10:9-10 confirms "That if you confess with your mouth, 'Jesus is Lord' and believe in your heart that God raised him from the dead, you will be saved. For it is with your heart that you believe and are justified, and it is with your mouth that you confess and are saved."

Now is the time to be saved. NOW! Right now! You never know when your time on earth is over. And after that, it is too late to be saved. Postponing this decision could result in hell forever. "Today, if you will hear His voice, do not harden your hearts." (Hebrews 3:7) "Behold, now is the accepted time; behold now is the day of salvation." (2 Corinthians 6:2b)

Jesus is the only way to be saved!

God's Word makes it clear. "Salvation is found in no one else, for there is no other name under heaven given to men by which we must be saved." (Acts 4:12) Jesus said: "Here I am! I stand at the door and knock. If anyone hears my voice and opens the door, I will come in and eat with him, and he with me." (Revelation 3:20)

God wants to, and will, forgive and save you if you ask, confess and yield. You can begin, or renew, a relationship with Him today. Let His love flow into your life to displace the fear. Let Him begin to produce the Fruit of the Spirit in and through your life.

Your salvation experience may not be as dramatic as mine and it may take some time to discern God's voice. That is fine. According to the Bible, it is impossible to experience salvation or repentance and stay the same. In other words, when we ask, confess, and yield, the Holy Spirit begins to bring glory to God by revealing His work in and through our lives.

Prayer is talking to God!

This is a sample prayer you could use. "Dear God, I realize and agree with you that I am a sinner. I know that I cannot save myself. I believe you sent Jesus to live a perfect life and offer it in payment for my sins. I ask you to forgive me. I ask you to save my soul. I yield control of my life to you and want you to make whatever changes need to be made. Thank you for loving me and providing a way for me to be saved and know you. Thank you for your Word and for the Holy Spirit. In Jesus' name I pray. Amen."

Meet your new family!

It is very important to contact a local Bible-believing and Bible-preaching church. Ask people you work with and live close to. You will want to let others know what has happened. Learn about the importance of baptism and church membership. God has provided a family for His born again children, brothers and sisters in Christ. I am so grateful for the impact of being baptized and membership with First Baptist Church of Columbia, Tennessee. I still carry my baptism certificate in my briefcase.

In a local church I found fellowship. I learned to study my Bible and to enjoy worship. What a difference it made to know I was accepted and loved! God provided guidance needed in learning to witness, pray and serve as my new brothers and sisters in Christ invited me to join them. My purpose in God's Kingdom was revealed while on my journey of faith. I finally found my place in this world.

Get to know the new you!

Learning our identity in Christ, through God's promises, produces freedom from shameful failures in the past and encourages growth. Receiving and giving forgiveness is part of that process. God created each of us with a need to know we are accepted, secure and significant. By His design, only He can meet those needs. Writing each of the following verses from the Bible on index cards and carrying them with me made a huge difference in the level of peace in my life. When I experienced rejection, I would read out loud the verses about being accepted by God. When I experienced uncertainty, I would read out loud the verses about security in God. When I questioned my value, I read out loud the verses about my significance to God.

There are many references to God's Word in the Bible. Ephesians 6:17 describes it as "the sword of the Spirit." I strongly encourage and challenge you to find in your Bible each verse listed. Write each one looking for a particular verse that you connect with, in each of the three sections. Carry those written verses with you. When you begin to think or feel rejection, read the verse about being accepted by God to yourself out loud. When you begin to think or feel insecure, read the verse about our security in Christ to yourself out loud. When you begin to think or feel you lack value, read the verse about significance to yourself out loud. Only God's Word can bring rest for your soul. When I give attention to

God's Word with my mind, eyes, mouth and ears, He uses it in my time of need.

Who we are in *CHRIST*

We are accepted:

God forgives us based on the finished work of Jesus.

"He made him who had no sin to be sin for us, so that in him we might become the righteousness of God." (2 Corinthians 5:21)

God accepts us as His children.

"Yet to all who received him, to those who believed in his name, he gave the right to become children of God- children born not of natural descent, nor of human decision or a husband's will, but born of God." (John 1:12, 13)

We have a home and citizenship beyond this world, in heaven.

"But our citizenship is in heaven. And we eagerly await a Savior from there, the Lord Jesus Christ." (Philippians 3:20)

We can be Jesus' friend.

"You are my friends if you do what I command." (John 15:14)

We can have peace with God now.

"Therefore, since we have been justified through faith, we have peace with God through our Lord Jesus Christ, through whom we have gained access by faith into this grace in which we now stand." (Romans 5:1)

We will never be rejected by God.

"I give them eternal life, and they shall never perish; no one can snatch them out of my hand. My Father, who has given them to me, is greater than all; no one can snatch them out of my Father's hand. " (John 10:28, 29)

We are secure:

We are more secure than we can comprehend.

"Who shall separate us from the love of Christ? Shall trouble or hardship or persecution or famine or nakedness or danger or sword? No, in all these things we are more than conquerors through him who loved us. For I am convinced that neither death nor life, neither angels nor demons, neither the present nor the future, nor any powers, neither height nor depth, nor anything else in all of creation will be able to separate us from the love of God that is in Christ Jesus our Lord." (Romans 8:35, 37-39)

We no longer have to live in fear.

"For God has not given us a spirit of fear and timidity, but of power, love and self-discipline." (2 Timothy 1:7)

God will finish the good work he has begun in our lives.

"… being confident of this, that he who began a good work in you will carry it on to completion until the day of Jesus Christ." (Philippians 1:6)

We are free from condemnation.

"Therefore, there is now no condemnation for those who are in Christ Jesus, because through Christ Jesus the law of the Spirit of life set me free from the law of sin and death." (Romans 8:1-2)

We are significant:

God chose us.

"You did not choose me, but I chose you and appointed you to go and bear fruit – fruit that will last." (John 15:16)

We have value to God.

"But God demonstrates his own love for us in this: while we were still sinners, Christ died for us." (Romans 5:8)

We have a valuable position on God's team.

"Therefore, if anyone is in Christ, he is a new creation; the old has gone, the new has come! All this is from God, who reconciled us to himself through Christ and gave us the ministry of reconciliation: that God was reconciling the world to himself in Christ, not counting men's sins against them. And he has committed to us the message of reconciliation. We are therefore Christ's ambassadors." (2 Corinthians 5:17-20)

We are God's workmanship.

"For we are God's workmanship, created in Christ Jesus to do good works, which God prepared in advance for us to do." (Ephesians 2:10)

"You will keep in perfect peace him whose mind is steadfast, because he trusts in you." (Isaiah 26:3) "Finally, brothers, whatever is true, whatever is noble, whatever is right, whatever is pure, whatever is lovely, whatever is admirable – if anything is excellent or praiseworthy – think about such things. Whatever you have learned or received or heard from me, or seen in me – put it into practice. And the God of peace will be with you." (Philippians 4:8-9)

"Do not be conformed any longer to the pattern of this world, but be transformed by the renewing of your mind. Then you will be able to test and approve what God's will is – his good, pleasing and perfect will." (Romans 12:2)

It is easier to trust someone we know. I suggest you read the Gospel of John. Have a notebook and pen handy. In each verse answer two questions. First, what did I learn about Jesus from reading this verse? Second, what did I learn about how Jesus treats people from reading this verse? Why is this so important? "The Son is the radiance of God's glory and the exact representation of his being, sustaining all things through his powerful word." (Hebrews 1:3) Whatever you learn about Jesus and how He treats people tells you about God the Father and how He treats people!

God has chosen to reveal Himself and His love for us through His Word, the Bible. He has also chosen to reveal to us who we are as His children. Reading, knowing and believing these verses will increase our trust in God. It will also change our view of ourselves.

Chapter 7

How do we continue? How did I get unstuck by forgiving myself?

One of my favorite comments, when confronted about my attitude or behavior in the past, was, "I'm not hurting anybody but myself." As God began to shine light on my past, I realized that statement was far from true. I had hurt others.

I began to make a list of people who deserved to hear me say, "I'm sorry. I hope you will forgive." Some were owed restitution. I had to ask, "What do I owe you?" or "What will it take to make this right?" I found each time that God provided the humility, courage, timing and words I needed to keep me from being defensive or causing more damage. While the responses were as varied as the people, I had to take ownership of the damage. I felt regret and deep sorrow that had previously been masked by anger. My shame, guilt and anger began to grow. Due to emotional exhaustion, I became discouraged and depressed.

I was spiritually taken captive as a prisoner of war. I realized that, even though I had asked God to forgive me for past sins, I had not forgiven myself.

Consequences of Not Forgiving Myself

Satan took advantage of this opportunity to convince me that, even though God had forgiven me, I could not forgive myself. Believing that lie, I was spiritually taken captive as a prisoner of war. I did not know I was in bondage until God used His Word to expose the deception. "The god of this age has blinded the minds of unbelievers, so that they cannot see the light of the gospel of the glory of Christ, who is in the image of God." (2 Corinthians 4:4)

You may be wondering about consequences I experienced because of believing the lie and not forgiving myself.

- I wasted precious emotional energy through fear, anger, pain, sadness and blame.
- I was a prisoner of the past, bound by feelings of vulnerability and insecurity.
- I went back to living in a reactive mode.
- My physical and emotional health was compromised.
- I went back to trying to be perfect, fearing failure.
- I went back to critically judging myself and others.
- I went back to hating myself.
- I went back to being controlled by opinions of others, with a fear of rejection.
- I went back to a cycle of self-destruction.
- I stopped progressing into the person of faith God wanted me to become.
- I became restless, dissatisfied and felt alone.

The rescue mission God used to deliver me came through His Word.

Even though I was discouraged and depressed, I continued to read my Bible. I was reminded that God loves and accepts me. He loved me too much to allow me to remain prisoner of war. The rescue mission God used to deliver me from this bondage came through His Word.

In 1 Corinthians 4:3-5 was the truth God used to confront the lie. In this passage the Apostle Paul is writing in response to the information he received about the church at Corinth. They had passed judgment on him. The passage didn't make sense to me at first. I kept reading it over and over. I knew there was a reason it held my attention. It seemed I couldn't stop thinking about it.

In that passage, the Holy Spirit led Paul to write, "I care very little if I am judged by you or by any human court; indeed, I do not even judge myself. My conscience is clear, but that does not make me innocent. It is the Lord who judges me. Therefore judge nothing before the appointed time; wait till the Lord comes. He will bring to light what is hidden in darkness and will expose the motives of men's hearts." Reread that again as much as you want, then I'll share a method I use to grow closer to God in His Word.

Done?

In this method, I break a passage into a list of sentences. This process of closer examination allows me to process and meditate on small portions of truth, one at a time. This is how it works for me:

- I don't care if you judge me.
- I don't care if any human court judges me.
- I do not even judge myself.

- My conscience is clear.
- I am not innocent.
- The Lord judges me.
- Judge nothing before the appointed time.
- Wait for the Lord to judge.
- God will bring what is hidden in darkness into the light.
- God will expose the motives of men's hearts.

God is the only one who has the authority to judge.

This passage of Scripture clearly states that God is the only one who has the authority to judge. Since God is the only one who has the authority to judge, I don't have the authority to judge myself. Nor do I have the authority to question, negate or overrule God's verdict. I have a choice. I will either agree, by depending on faith, or disagree by depending on what I feel and what makes sense to me. If I disagree I will be in the sin of unbelief.

We know the Holy Spirit would never put thoughts in our mind that contradict Scripture. So, if I am judging myself, it is clearly not the Holy Spirit putting those thoughts in my mind and leading me to that conclusion. <u>To trust God is a faith-based process, not a process of feelings or logic.</u> Why did Paul forgive himself? Why do I forgive myself? Because the truth is we have been forgiven.

The Benefits of Forgiving Yourself

You may want to know some of the benefits of agreeing with God by faith and forgiving myself.

- I have realized how important it is to trust God enough to agree with Him.
- I have been spared the stress and pain of living in false guilt.

- I have more faith in God and less trust in my emotions and logic.
- I understand better God's expectations of me.
- God has delivered me from the trap of needing to please people.
- My identity in Christ continues to bring comfort and confidence.
- I now see and treat myself as a forgiven person.
- God is helping me accept myself the way He made me.
- God has given me permission to laugh and to heal.
- God is helping me to take better care of myself, spiritually, mentally, emotionally and physically.
- I have a clear conscience.
- I am embracing forgiveness as a lifetime journey.

You may be thinking that you can't do all this. Remember: "that he who began a good work in you will carry it on to completion until the day of Christ Jesus." (Philippians 1:6b) It is the Holy Spirit's responsibility to bring glory to God by transforming and equipping me to live by faith.

Have you agreed with God by accepting your forgiveness? If not, here is a sample prayer:

"Dear God,

Thank you for the faith to believe the truth of Your Word. I need courage, wisdom and strength to put the faith you have given me to work. Thank you that the Bible says when I confess my sins to you and ask for your forgiveness, you are faithful to Your Word and will forgive me. Once again, I ask you to forgive me of the sins I have committed. I choose by faith to agree with you that I am forgiven by forgiving myself. Please help me to rest in Your character, Your Word and Your love. In Jesus' name I pray. Amen."

Chapter 8

How do we finish the process? How did God lead me to forgive others?

After I asked God to forgive me, the weight of guilt and shame began to lift and was replaced with peace, hope and relief. Looking back, I saw it was nothing short of a miracle of God's grace and mercy. This is a common miracle among both new believers and repentant believers. It happens when we choose to act on the faith God provides to process the debt others owe. I had also gone through the process of recognizing the difference between conviction of the Holy Spirit and false guilt from Satan. I had forgiven myself, by faith, agreeing with God that I was forgiven.

God was dealing with me about forgiving other people.

Soon after all this took place, it seemed like every time I opened my Bible, I saw a verse about forgiveness. God was dealing with me about forgiving other people. Some people were easier to forgive than others. There was one person I wasn't ready or willing to forgive: my father. I told God that I didn't want any part in forgiving my dad. I loved my dad, probably to keep from hating him. I did hate the impact of my dad's choices in my life and the lives of our family. From my point of view, my dad's choices had taken away many of my choices.

My parents divorced when I was a small child and I grew up without my dad being involved in my life. From my perspective, if my dad had been walking with God, many of the negative life-shaping events and experiences that happened to me could have been avoided. All the bad choices that children of divorce can make, I made. I struggled with why my dad was gone. After I started to school, I struggled with why our family was not like other families.

I will always be grateful for the love, grace and sacrifices that my grandparents made while my mother, my sisters, and I lived with them for five years. After my mother remarried, I struggled with how different my stepdad was from my grandfather. Our grandparents were very affectionate and verbally expressed love for us. My stepdad wasn't that way, so I thought there was something wrong with me rather than with him. I often struggled with anxiety and anger because it seemed I was always saying something wrong or doing something wrong. I always felt like I was a problem for someone.

Our mother did the best she knew to do with the resources available. Her life and dreams had been shattered. Her children had been deeply wounded. She would live much of her life searching for an answer to the "why" question. It would be more than 50 years before she forgave my dad. And I'm so thankful she did.

From the five years we lived with extended family, I have many good memories, but I was also exposed to some things that children aren't supposed to know about or see. On occasion there was drinking and things got kind of crazy and wild.

I made a lot of bad choices and was on the wrong end of some other people's choices. I was introduced to sexuality, drinking and smoking cigarettes as a child. These became opportunities for my long-term destruction as these vices became very powerful forces in my life. These vices were a way to change my feelings, to escape the anger and anxiety for a little while, and to self-medicate.

I struggled with my resentment toward my stepdad and my stepmom after both parents remarried. I just wanted us to be normal; I often felt they kept us from being a normal family. I often felt disconnected, like something was wrong with me. I hated being angry, feeling guilty and insecure, but I didn't know how to not be that way.

I spent a lot of time trying to understand why my dad said he loved me, but was not involved in my life. This searching only added to my struggles.

God knew my struggle was genuine.

I told God that I wanted my dad to get on his knees and ask me for forgiveness. God knew my struggle was genuine. He accepted me where I was in the process, but loved me too much to leave me stuck in destruction and bondage. God knew the process I was going through was a normal, necessary and genuine process even though I didn't know it at the time.

Again, it seemed as if every time I opened my Bible there was something about forgiveness jumping off the page to confront me. I prayed, asking God to show me the truth and to give me the desire, faith, courage and wisdom to trust him with the next step in this process. One day, as I was reading Romans 12:19, my prayer was answered. The verse says, "Do not take revenge, my friends, but leave room for God's wrath, for it is written: 'It is mine to avenge; I will repay,' says the Lord." God was saying to me, "Mike, your dad hasn't gotten away with anything. He is going to stand before me one day and answer for all he has done, just like everybody else. You have my Word, either I'll settle up with him or I'm a liar." I knew that God was not a liar.

God then said, "Mike, have I made available to you the faith you need to trust me with the debt your dad owes you?" I thought about that question for a few minutes and then realized that everything God tells us to do, He has to give us the faith to do it.

The message God was telling me?

Until you forgive, I can't heal you or release you.

"Mike, until you forgive I can't heal you or release you from those events that continue to cause anger and hurt. Forgiveness isn't going to change your relationship with your dad. It is going to change your relationship with me." Then I understood that <u>forgiveness is an act of faith, in obedience to God</u>, in which we turn the debt over to God to collect.

To be candid, I had no desire to forgive my dad. I didn't feel like forgiving him. It didn't make sense, logically, to forgive him. But my choice became clear: obey God by faith or disobey Him and sin.

Forgiving my dad that day didn't change my relationship with my dad, but it did change my relationship with my Heavenly Father. Becoming like Jesus in my willingness to forgive will be a lifelong journey, but forgiving my dad put me back on the road in my journey toward forgiveness and peace.

Most people have a situational dictionary and vocabulary. Their "no" is no to some people but to others, "no" could mean maybe. "Fine" is not the same to everyone. To one person "fine" means I'm okay, but to another person it means "whatever." Yet to another, fine means "just forget it." The situational dictionary and vocabulary produce miscommunication and misunderstanding in relationships.

For this reason it is essential we know from God's Word the true meaning of forgive. While God expects us to learn, He also requires us to act upon what we learn. Our understanding of God's true meaning of forgive requires us to follow through to complete the process. In other words, knowledge is not enough. <u>Action is required</u>.

Webster's Dictionary defines "forgive" as: "1. To grant pardon for or remission of (something); cease to demand the penalty for. 2. To grant freedom from penalty to (someone); 3. To cease to blame or feel resentment against. 4. To remit, as a debt." (Webster's Dictionary of the English Language, 1992 J. G. Ferguson Publishing Company, Chicago, Illinois, p. 381)

God's Word defines "forgive" as: acknowledging and turning the debt over to God, with the promise that He will "avenge, He will repay." (Romans 12:19)

To forgive, from God's perspective, is an act of faith.

To forgive, from God's perspective, is an act of faith. To forgive does not require that I feel like forgiving. I have heard people say "if I don't feel it in my heart, it isn't real." Not true! To forgive does not require that I feel anything or that it make sense. To forgive is to yield to God's command by faith, regardless of whether I feel like forgiving or regardless of whether it makes sense to forgive.

NO AMOUNT OF REVENGE CAN REPLACE WHAT WAS LOST!

God's Word is very clear regarding our willingness to forgive. Matthew 7:1-2: "Do not judge, or you too will be judged. For in the same way you judge others, you will be judged, and with the measure you use, it will be measured to you." (Matthew 7:1-2)

> *If there is someone you have not yet forgiven,*
> *let me suggest this prayer.*

"Dear God,

I ask you to forgive me for disobeying your Word and not forgiving others. I thank you that you have made available to me the faith needed to forgive _____. I choose to accept that faith as a gift and to agree and obey you by turning over to you the debt owed to me by _____. Thank you that you can be trusted to settle this debt and that I don't have to remain stuck in this process anymore. Please give me wisdom to understand how you want me to deal with what happened and with the person who hurt me. In Jesus' name I pray. Amen."

Chapter 9

No Forgiveness = No Peace;
Know Forgiveness = Know Peace.

I love the following quotes about forgiveness.

"I think that if God forgives us we must forgive ourselves. Otherwise, it is almost like setting up ourselves as a higher tribunal than Him." C.S. Lewis

"It's not just other people we need to forgive. We also need to forgive ourselves. For all the things we didn't do. All the things we should have done." Mitch Albom, Tuesdays with Morrie

"God has left sin in the world in order that there may be forgiveness: not only the secret forgiveness by which He Himself cleanses our souls, but the manifest forgiveness by which we have mercy on one another and so give expression to the fact that He is living, by His mercy, in our own hearts." Thomas Merton.

"It's not an easy journey, to get to a place where you forgive people. But it is such a powerful place, because it frees you." Tyler Perry

Are you up to date in asking God to forgive you?

If your answer is yes, praise the Lord! If your answer is no, I would strongly encourage you to take care of that now. You can read Section II and Chapter 6 again. Also, remember the Holy Spirit would never put the thought in your mind to postpone asking God to forgive you.

Forgiveness leads to a godly peace. We need to be forgiven daily. Thankfully, when we ask God to forgive us, He will do it, every time, every minute of every day.

"If we confess our sins, he is faithful and just and will forgive us our sins and purify us from all unrighteousness." (1 John 1:9)

It is essential that I allow God to define sin. God's Word says: "Whatever is not of faith is sin." (Romans 14:23b) "Everyone who sins breaks the law; in fact, sin is lawlessness." (1 John 3:4)

God's Word says that we must make faith-based decisions as we surrender to the Lordship of Jesus and leadership of the Holy Spirit, through Scripture.

Are you up to date in forgiving yourself?

If your answer is yes, praise the Lord! If your answer is no, I would strongly encourage you to take care of that now. You can read Section II and Chapter 7 again. Also, remember that the Holy Spirit would never put the thought in your mind to postpone forgiving yourself.

"I care very little if I am judged by you or any human court; I do not even judge myself. My conscience is clear, but that does not make me innocent. It is the Lord who judges me. Therefore judge nothing before the appointed time; wait until the Lord comes. He will bring to light what is hidden in darkness and will expose the motives of the heart. At that time each will receive their praise from God." (1 Corinthians 4:3-5)

Is there anyone you have not yet forgiven?

If your answer is no, praise the Lord! If your answer is yes, I would strongly encourage you to take care of that now. You can read again Section II and Chapter 8 of this book. Also, remember that the Holy Spirit would never put the thought in your mind to postpone forgiving others. Chapter 8 provides the definition of what forgiveness means and doesn't mean.

God wants us to know peace more than we want to. But He is only going to offer it to us on His terms. His terms reflect His deep love for us. "For if you forgive other people when they sin against you, your heavenly Father will also forgive you. But if you do not forgive others their sins, your Father will not forgive your sins." (Matthew 6:14-15) "And when you stand praying, if you hold anything against anyone, forgive them, so that your Father in heaven may forgive you your sins." (Mark 11:25) "Be kind and compassionate to one another, forgiving each other, just as in Christ God forgave you." (Ephesians 4:32) "Bear with each other and forgive one another if any of you has a grievance against someone. Forgive as the Lord forgave you." (Colossians 3:13)

Chapter 10

Can God use my journey?

The first eight years in my journey of forgiveness were a time of healing, discovery and learning. Most of what is used in the Biblical counseling ministry, Hope Family Ministries, comes from the lessons I learned during that eight years and beyond.

> ***God has not wasted anything that***
> ***has happened in my life.***

"Praise be to the God and Father of our Lord Jesus Christ, the Father of compassion and the God of all comfort, who comforts us in all our troubles, so that we can comfort those in any trouble with the comfort we ourselves have received from God." (2 Corinthians 1:3-4)

At a time when I was really struggling with the events of my life, I asked God, "Why have you allowed me to go through all these things?" What I understood Him to say was,

"If you had not been hurt and healed, you could not help people who are hurting."

It is powerful when we realize someone understands what we are going through from personal experience. God has used the suffering in my life to connect with others who are struggling. This helps them to feel understood and accepted in abnormal circumstances.

It is not that I have sought out people to help. God is using what He has done in my life as He brings people across my path. It is my job to walk by faith. It is His job to live His life through me.

God let me know that change was on the way.

In 1994 and 1995, through a series of events, God let me know that change was coming. I had lost my passion and interest in the skilled trade I had worked for many years. My focus had shifted to the people around me. People were approaching me at work, at church and in the neighborhood – all seeking advice.

All I knew to do was to try to find common ground between us and to point to a story in Scripture that related to their problem. It was common for people to tell me they were confused and were struggling with hope. While nothing changed in their circumstances, they saw things from a different perspective. This gave them hope and a better understanding of what the next prayer or step might be. I really had no idea that I was counseling people. If you had told me that is what I was doing, I would have said I wasn't trained or qualified to counsel. Yet people who got better told other people where they found help.

I began to see that the Lord was using me to help others deal with the problems in their lives.

During this time period, I attended several Christian events, such as Promise Keepers rallies. My wife and I also attended a marriage retreat during the New Year's holiday, 1994-1995. In March 1995, I attended a powerful three-day Christian retreat called The Walk to Emmaus. It was a time of fellowship, worship and learning, away from the distractions of daily life. God drew me closer and challenged me to renew my surrender to His call on my life. He impressed upon me that change was coming. All I knew for sure was that I wouldn't be a machinist/tool and die maker much longer. I had no idea what I would be or where things were headed, but I had an amazing peace about the whole process.

I was willing to do whatever God wanted me to do.

I sought guidance and prayer from my pastor several times during this period. All I knew to tell Him was that I was willing to do whatever God wanted me to do. He kept assuring me that God would make it clear.

Sometime in early 1995, I had an accident at work that required surgery. I was off work for three weeks and then placed on light duty with a lifting restriction. During those three weeks, I prayed and studied the Bible. God impressed upon me that He wanted me to be available to help people find hope and direction during their challenging times.

I went to my Sunday School teacher, Mr. Robert Upchurch, and asked for prayer and suggestions. He encouraged me, agreed to pray for me and suggested I see a local attorney, Greg Pirkle, who specializes in tax-related issues. I had no idea what to say other than what God had impressed upon me and laid upon my heart. He heard me out and encouraged me, saying that he had seen a need for this service in our community. He suggested we pray about setting up a non-profit agency. This would allow people to participate in the work. He told me to pray about six people to serve as board members and to pray about a name for the ministry.

About this time, a friend, Jim Nolting, told me two things that had an impact on me. He said, "Mike, God has plenty of machinists and tool and die makers. He needs you to be available to help His people." He also told me, "Mike, if you will let people know what God is doing, they will support your work."

We set up the non-profit agency, Hope Family Ministries, with six original Board Members. Those first Board Members included: Robert and Joann Upchurch, Merrill and Ellen Johnston, and Jim and Carol Nolting. They and many other people have faithfully prayed and continued to support the ministry.

I had a very strong conviction about several things associated with the ministry. First, we would provide service on a donation basis. If those we counseled wanted to help us, they could, but we would not require payment nor ask about ability to pay. Second, the Bible and God's plan for reconciliation would be our primary foundation. We would, in grace and love, share God's truth without being judgmental or softening God's plan for our journey of faith. Third, our counselors would be Biblical counselors, not psycho-therapists.

Our objectives, in counseling, remain:

1. We will come alongside each person and help them see where they are stuck. Everybody except Jesus has been stuck in processing life.

2. We will encourage and equip that person as they go through their season so that they have a clear conscience and grow in faith.

As of this date, March 31, 2014, we have provided Biblically-based counseling for 18¾ years. During that period of time, we have experienced:

Biblical counseling hours:	37,064
People counseled:	12,167
Marriages counseled:	6,392
Prayed to surrender life to Jesus:	2,207
Prayed to rededicate life to Jesus:	4,652
Workshop attendance:	8,368

To God be the glory!
Amen!

Additional information about Hope Family Ministries is available. Please contact us:

Hope Family Ministries
2754 Mattox Street
Tupelo, MS 38801
(662) 842-4673
Hopefamilyministries.com

Epilogue

The Most Important Thing I've Learned about the Fruit of the Spirit

When I first came to know the Lord, I was a machinist/tool & die maker. So I was used to reading blue prints and using precision tools to measure. As I began to read my Bible, therefore, my mindset was to look for the "blueprint," or the big picture of how I could measure progress and failure.

Hebrew 11:6 told me that "without faith it is impossible to please God." I realized that I had to know what faith was and how to know if I am "in faith."

My workplace had two groups of skilled craftsmen. An apprentice is one who has not yet learned the trade and worked the number of hours to complete the apprenticeship. A journeyman is one who has successfully learned the trade and has completed the hours of apprenticeship. If you want tried and true knowledge, don't ask an apprentice, ask a journeyman.

I began to look around in the church for some journeyman Christians to ask, "What does it mean to walk by faith? How do you know when you are in faith and not in faith?" One said, "Mike, that means you have to trust God with your money. You need to tithe and help people as you can." Another said, "You have to be a witness for the Lord. You have to share the gospel and help people find their place in the church." A third said, "According to the book of James, you have to keep yourself unpolluted from the world and help take care of the widows and orphans."

As I walked away from the third conversation I thought, *I can't see how to connect those answers with the two questions.* People who don't know God can give money to the church and to the less fortunate. People who don't know God can share the good news of the gospel. People who don't know God can live a moral life and help take care of the widows and orphans.

So I began to read my Bible and to ask God to show me how to know when I am in faith and when I am not in faith. I found answers in the book of Galatians, which addresses the new covenant and freedom in Christ. Chapter 5 was especially helpful as I read about comparing the fruit of the flesh to the Fruit of the Spirit. God impressed upon me, "Mike, Satan can portray himself as an angel of light, but he cannot counterfeit the Fruit of the Spirit. The way you know if you are in faith is whether or not I am putting the Fruit of the Spirit in your life."

My understanding of how the Holy Spirit gives us His fruit, through faith, has helped me help hundreds of people in my counseling ministry.

I want to give you a tool that has proven very helpful to me, in many situations. I've borrowed this wisdom from a booklet, "Have You Made the Wonderful Discovery of the Spirit-Filled Life?", produced by Campus Crusade for Christ.

Please consider Illustration A below, and tell me what you see in the circle. Don't analyze or interpret it, just tell me one thing you see in the circle.

There is a chair. There is an S. There is a cross. There are dots.

Illustration A

- Legalistic attitude
- Impure thoughts
- Jealousy
- Guilt
- Worry
- Discouragement
- Critical spirit
- Frustration
- Aimlessness

- Fear
- Ignorance of one's spiritual heritage
- Unbelief
- Disobedience
- Loss of love for God and for others
- Poor prayer life
- No desire for Bible study

Now look at the list on the left side of the circle. Which of those are happening in your life now? Take time to reflect over the past week.

This illustration represents a born again believer who is not trusting God with one thing or more. Because of that, Jesus has been dethroned, which is why the cross is not in the chair.

When Jesus is dethroned, by default, self or the sin nature gets back in the chair and tries to run things. The dots, out of order, represents chaos or disorder.

The list on the left side of the circle, according to Galatians, is included in something called the fruit of the flesh.

What is the four-letter word on the right side, at the top? *Fear.*

Whenever Christ is not on the throne of our lives, fear becomes our chief motivator. Satan's goal, every minute of every day, is to for us to live in Illustration A. He knows that God has told us, over 365 times, in the Bible, to not live in fear. But when we are trying to control our own lives, when we are on the throne of our own lives, fear is all we have.

Now, consider Illustration B, below.

Tell me what you see that is different from the first illustration.

The cross is in the chair. The S is not in the chair. The dots are in order.

Look at the list on the left side of the circle.

It is quite different from the first illustration, isn't it?

It is, according to Galatians 5, the Fruit of the Spirit.

Illustration B

- Love
- Joy
- Peace
- Patience
- Kindness
- Goodness
- Faithfulness
- Gentleness
- Self-control

- Life is Christ-centered
- Empowered by Holy Spirit
- Introduces others to Christ
- Has effective prayer life
- Understands God's word
- Trusts God
- Obeys God

This illustrates a born again believer who is trusting God enough to get out of Illustration A.

When we keep Christ on the throne of our lives, we are being motivated or controlled by faith.

God's desire is that we live by faith, that we trust Him with everything, both big and small, that comes our way.

Illustration A = fear. Illustration B = faith.

Satan wants us to focus on what we feel. He also wants us to analyze what is going on around us and try to weigh the options and predict the outcome.

God gave us emotions and the ability to reason and think. But he also told us to not let either of those have more power than His Word.

While we have little or no control over the circumstances we are exposed to, we do have a choice about how we respond to those circumstances.

If we shift our focus from what is happening to <u>how</u> we are responding to what is happening, are we responding in fear or in faith?

If we respond in faith, God will give us courage, wisdom and strength in the exact measure needed.

Hebrews 11:6 states that "without faith it is impossible to please God."

2 Cor. 5:9 the apostle Paul says "we make it our goal to please Him."

If we make it our goal to please God, by putting faith to work, we must trust God with everything. To go from Illustration B (the fruit of the spirit) to Illustration A (fear), all I have to do is not trust God with one thing.

It seems simple. And it is, this path of trusting God with absolutely everything that comes our way in life. But it is how

He provides for us. He knows that we can't handle anything on our own, even with the gifts and aptitudes He has given us.

I can safely say that I have no great wisdom to give to the people who come to Hope Family Ministries for counseling. I do, however, have access to the greatest wisdom that ever was and ever will be – the wisdom from God that He promises to give to those who trust in Him.

Are you troubled? Read the scripture I've listed in this book. Learn from my mistakes as I've grown in the Lord and experienced His peace.

And turn it over to God, through Christ, whatever it is that's troubling you.

Referring to His disciples, Jesus said: "Thus, by their fruit you will recognize them." (Matthew 7:20)   The way I use illustrations A and B is by checking every 30 minutes (on the hour and half hour) to see what kind of fruit is showing. My prayer is "Lord, how am I doing?" If I find myself back in illustration A, I don't let the devil beat me up about it. I just say "Lord, I give it all back to you." If I find myself still in illustration B, I say "Thank you, Lord. Let's go another 30 minutes." Also, every 30 minutes I pray specifically for the thing that weighs heaviest on me.

As I understand it, it is our job as God's children, to stay in illustration B. It is God's job to live His life through us. Do I stay in illustration B perfectly? No! Jesus, while here in earthly form, stayed in illustration B perfectly. God wants us to live in the present moment, in His presence. That is the only place we will experience the abundant life. God wants us to rest in our souls about Him and ourselves because when we trust Him enough to do that, He brings glory to Himself.

He is worthy of your trust. He cares for you. Remember, God knows what He is doing and He really can be trusted!

Acknowledgements

So many people have contributed to this book, some without even realizing it. I want to thank:

Those who loved me when I was not an easy person to love: my mother, sister and grandparents (maw and pop); my wife and son of 35 years, who saw something in me that was good, who stirred the desire and willingness to make better choices, who endured our first 7 years (before Jesus changed me), who have paid the price of accepting God's call to my vocational change, years of education and a life of faith; my daughter in law and grandchildren, who love and respect me more than I'll ever deserve; my wife's family, who have accepted and loved me like family in the good and bad times.

Those who believed God could change and use a guy like me: those who chose to be a friend; those who helped me learn a skilled trade and become a craftsman;

Those who mentored me as a new Christian teaching me to study my Bible, pray, serve and witness; those who heard my story, burden and vision to help others and chose to participate; those who have prayed, donated time, money and things the ministry needed; those who have served on our Board of Directors; those who are Hope's Heroes; those who found hope and peace through counseling at HFM and told someone else.

To Jesus, who paid the price for my sin and offered me forgiveness and eternal life.

To God for never giving up on me and proving He can take anyone and use them however He sees fit.

To the Holy Spirit for continuing to patiently and consistently finish the good work He has started in my life.